NEW THEORIES ON
DIET AND NUTRITION

NEW THEORIES ON DIET AND NUTRITION

SALLY LEE

FRANKLIN WATTS
NEW YORK LONDON TORONTO SYDNEY
] 1990 [

Photographs courtesy of: Rothco Cartoons: pp. 8 (Wicks/The Newhall Signal, CA), 74 (Glasbergen), 143 (Schwadron); Stock, Boston: pp. 11 (Peter Menze), 46 (George Malave), 50 (Elizabeth Crews), 66 (Jeff Albertson), 83 (Frank Siteman), 94 (Jean-Claude Lejeune), 106 (Dean Abramson); Taurus Photos: pp. 16 (Martin M. Rotker/Science Photo Library International), 18 and 63 (Martin M. Rotker), 99 (Shirley Zeiberg); Medichrome/The Stock Shop, Inc.: pp. 17 (L. Moskowitz), 21 and 22 (both, Tom Raymond), 71 (Ken Lax); Monkmeyer Press: pp. 26 (Michal Heron), 102 (Bill Anderson), 126 (Mimi Forsyth); Peter Arnold: p. 41 (Laura Dwight); Phototake: p. 68 (CNRI); American Cancer Society: p. 78; Photo Researchers: p. 88 (Susan Rosenberg); Randy Matesow: pp. 110, 131; National Dairy Council: p. 147 (all).

Library of Congress Cataloging-in-Publication Data

Lee, Sally
New theories on diet and nutrition/by Sally Lee.
p.   cm.
Includes bibliographical references.
Summary: Examines different nutrients and their effects on the body and discusses malnutrition, vitamin deficiencies, and other conditions which may occur if proper eating habits are not maintained.
ISBN 0-531-10930-5
1. Nutrition—Juvenile literature.   2. Nutrionally induced diseases—Juvenile literature.   [1. Nutrition.   2. Nutritionally induced diseases.]   I. Title.
RA784.L398   1990
613.2—DC20   89-39357   CIP   AC

CONTENTS

NEW THEORIES ON DIET AND NUTRITION

ONE

THE CHANGING AMERICAN DIET

It's hard even to imagine the pilgrims stopping off at McDonald's for a cheeseburger or popping a TV dinner into their microwave. Life-styles and diets were much different in colonial America, and they have been changing ever since that time.

In the early days of our country most people lived and worked in rural areas. Their meals consisted of the things they grew, caught, or traded for. Diets were made up mainly of breads, potatoes, vegetables from the garden, and whatever meat was available. Now the majority of our population lives in urban areas. Our foods are chosen from thousands of products sold at grocery stores and supermarkets. With more women in the work force and more single people living on their own, large family meals are becoming less common. People rely more on "fast foods" both in restaurants and at home.

Our diets have also been changed by technology. Advances in agriculture have brought about higher yields and foods of better quality. Once the food is harvested, it can be quickly transported to the consumer or processed in a number of ways to keep it safe. At one time most food was smoked, dried, or canned to preserve it. Today, fresh foods can be frozen, freeze-dried, sealed in vacuum pouches, dehydrated, pasteurized, or treated with special gases to prevent spoilage.

The new methods of growing and processing foods have improved the "shelf life" and increased the variety of foods we have access to. A grocery store in the 1920s may have stocked about 800 different items. Today's supermarkets carry some 23,000 products, including exotic fruits, vegetables, and imported delicacies. Many supermarkets contain delicatessens, seafood sections, bakeries, pharmacies, and other specialized departments.

The American diet is envied by most of the rest of the world. Our technology has made it possible for us to have plenty to eat all year round. Even families without a lot of money can find enough inexpensive foods to prevent most of the nutritional deficiencies that plague underdeveloped countries. Our normal diet contains foods that are considered delicacies in other parts of the world, such as meats, eggs, dairy products, ice cream, pastries, and some fried foods.

Unfortunately, living in such an affluent society does not guarantee that our diets are nutritionally sound. As nations become richer, their

*Tomatoes being processed in a cannery
in Modesto, California*

food choices generally expand. Although some of these changes are good, some are not. Americans are eating less today but are getting fatter because they are eating more fattening foods and engaging in less physical activity. Although we are eating about as much protein as before, this protein is now coming more from fatty meats than from grains. In addition, meals are often accompanied by an increased use of margarine and oils. In 1900, about 30 percent of the daily calories for most people came from fat. Today, this average has risen to 45 percent.

The American diet recently came under heavy attack from former surgeon general of the United States, C. Everett Koop. Koop verified what nutritionists have known for quite a while. America's nutritional health problems are a result of overnutrition rather than undernutrition. We eat too much, and too much of what we eat are the wrong things. In general, we take in too much cholesterol, saturated fat, total fat, calories, sugar, salt, and alcohol.

What we eat clearly affects our chances of developing at least one or more major diseases, including heart disease, stroke, osteoporosis, diabetes, and some types of cancer. These diseases account for over two-thirds of the deaths in the United States each year.

Since the 1970s, there has been a renewed interest in nutrition as a way of maintaining health. Before that, the focus was on advances in drug therapy as a way to deal with disease. Now, more people are becoming concerned about what they eat. They are realizing that the right diet will not only reduce their risks of developing serious diseases but will add to the quality of their lives.

Sadly, many of the people hoping to improve their health through good nutrition are being victimized by promoters who push false information and unnecessary, even dangerous, products on unwary consumers. Billions of dollars each year are spent on unsound weight-loss schemes, unnecessary vitamin supplements, and ineffective cures for various ailments. Sound nutritional education is needed in order to separate the sense from the nonsense. Unfortunately, this information often does not receive the same colorful headlines as misinformation does.

Much is still being learned in the field of nutrition. The knowledge gained through the testing of new theories can aid in adjusting diets in order to enhance life and health.

=TWO=

EATING FOR
A HEALTHY HEART

"The way to a man's heart is through his stomach," is an old adage advising single girls that they could capture their man by enticing him with good food. Today, it has a new meaning, for what goes into a man's (or woman's or child's) stomach may very well find its way to the heart, or at least the arteries surrounding it.

Heart disease is the number one killer in the United States. Each year more than 1.5 million people suffer from heart attacks. More than 550,000 of them die. Heart disease accounts for more deaths than all the forms of cancer put together.

There are several risk factors in the development of heart disease, and only some are related to diet. The most significant factors are high blood cholesterol, high blood pressure, and smoking. Other factors are heredity, obesity, lack of exercise,

diabetes, age, and stress. <u>The more risk factors a</u> ✸
<u>person has, the greater his or her chances are of</u>
<u>having a heart attack.</u> — Vocabulary + history

ATHEROSCLEROSIS

The most common form of heart disease is caused
by atherosclerosis (ATH-er-oh-scler-oh-sis), or
"hardening of the arteries." Atherosclerosis is a
progressive disease in which the lining of the arteries becomes coated with fatty substances such as
cholesterol.

Atherosclerosis develops slowly over the
years. Mounds of fat and cholesterol mixed with
smooth muscle cells and calcium form a material
called *plaque* that builds up inside the artery walls.
When the plaque becomes rough and uneven, it
snags more deposits of fat and cholesterol as they
pass through the artery. Eventually, the plaque
buildup narrows the opening through the artery
until the blood flow is reduced to a dribble.

Atherosclerosis is especially harmful when it
involves the coronary arteries, the arteries carrying
blood to the heart muscle. When these arteries
become so clogged that they cannot deliver
enough blood to the heart, it can trigger a sudden
heart attack and the death or slow destruction of
part of the heart muscle.

As the inner surface of the artery becomes
more jagged, blood clots may form. A clot traveling
through the bloodstream can plug up the narrow
opening of an artery, cutting off the blood flow.

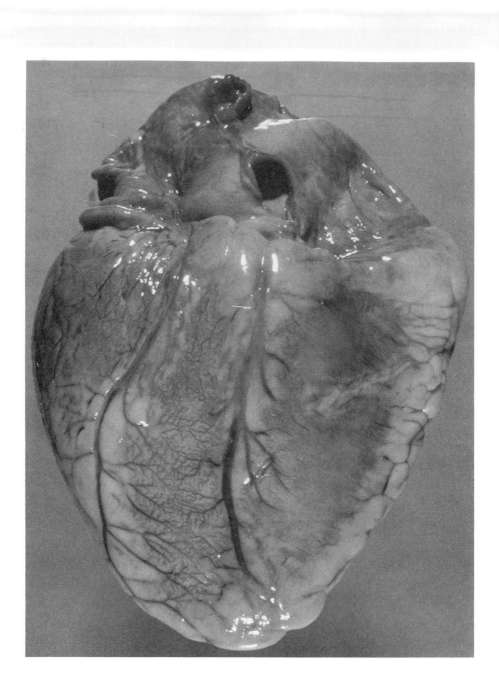

An anterior (frontal) view of a healthy human heart

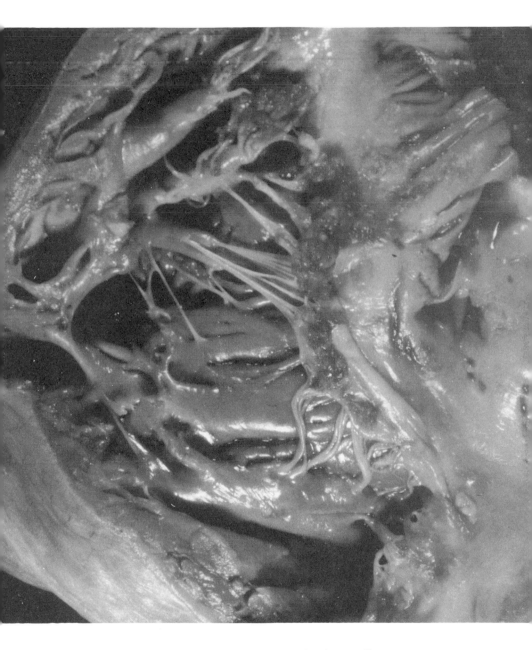

A heart severely damaged by heart disease

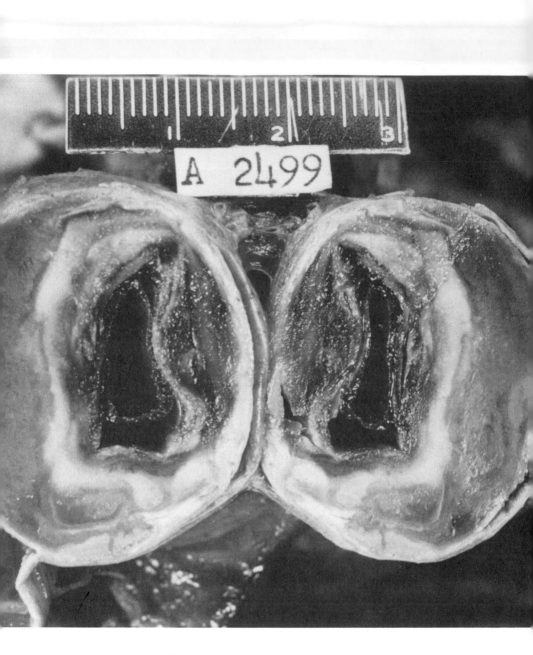

Cholesterol (white rings) lines the iliac
artery of this human heart.

When the blockage occurs in a coronary artery, a heart attack can result. When arteries in the head and neck are blocked, blood is kept from reaching the brain, causing a stroke.

CHOLESTEROL

The rate at which plaque builds up in the arteries depends primarily upon how much cholesterol piles up there. Cholesterol is a waxy substance made primarily in the liver. It is also found in foods *needs* of animal origin, such as meats and dairy prod- *+* ucts. Although we think of cholesterol as being *dairy* bad, our bodies need a certain amount of it. Cho- *products* lesterol is a part of all cell membranes and is needed to make sex hormones, vitamin D, and bile (which allows us to digest fats). Although cholesterol is important to the body, large amounts of it are not really needed in the diet because the liver makes a sufficient amount.

Scientists have known for years that cholesterol is an important element in the development of atherosclerosis. Now they are realizing that the way the cholesterol is transported through the blood is even more significant. Cholesterol doesn't travel through the blood freely. First, the body wraps it in a protein "package." This tiny glob of fat wrapped in protein is called a *lipoprotein*. Lipoproteins differ in the amount of cholesterol and other fats they carry and are identified by their densities. The ones we hear about the most are low-density lipoproteins (LDLs), sometimes referred to as "bad" cholesterol, and high-density lipoproteins (HDLs), also known as "good" cholesterol. There are also very low-density lipoproteins (VLDLs), which are eventually converted to LDLs.

LDLs, the main carriers of cholesterol, contain less protein and are more fragile than HDLs. As they race through the arteries carrying cholesterol to the cells, they may hit rough spots where plaque has begun to build up. On crashing, their cholesterol is strewn along the artery walls, adding to the accumulation of plaque.

Instead of being harmful, HDLs can actually help remove cholesterol from the body. As they travel through the arteries they "pick up" excess cholesterol and carry it back to the liver, where it is eventually excreted. People with high levels of HDLs in their blood have a lower risk of heart disease. In fact, some scientists believe that in certain cases of atherosclerosis, too little HDL may be as significant as too much LDL.

Serum (blood) *cholesterol* is measured by a blood test that tells how many milligrams of cholesterol are in a deciliter of blood (mg/dl). The risk of heart disease increases as cholesterol levels rise above 200 to 220 mg/dl. People with cholesterol over 265 mg/dl have four times the risk of developing heart disease as do those with a level of 190 mg/dl or lower.

Blood tests can also tell how much of the cholesterol is made up of HDLs. Normal HDL levels are 45 to 50 for men and 50 to 60 for women.

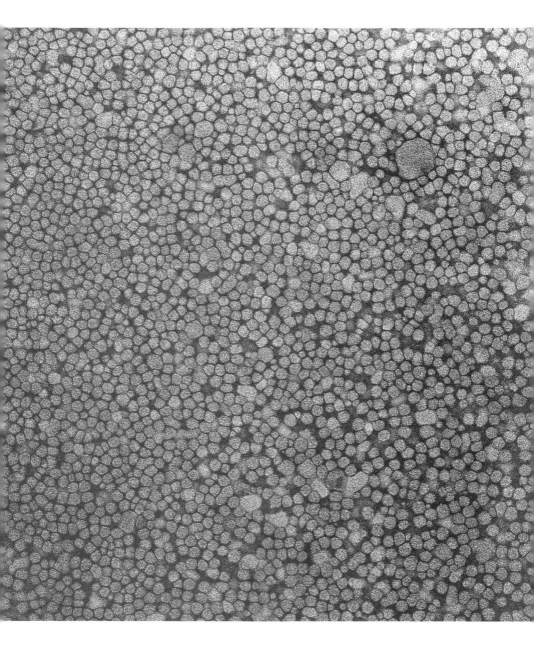

LDLs, the "bad" lipoproteins

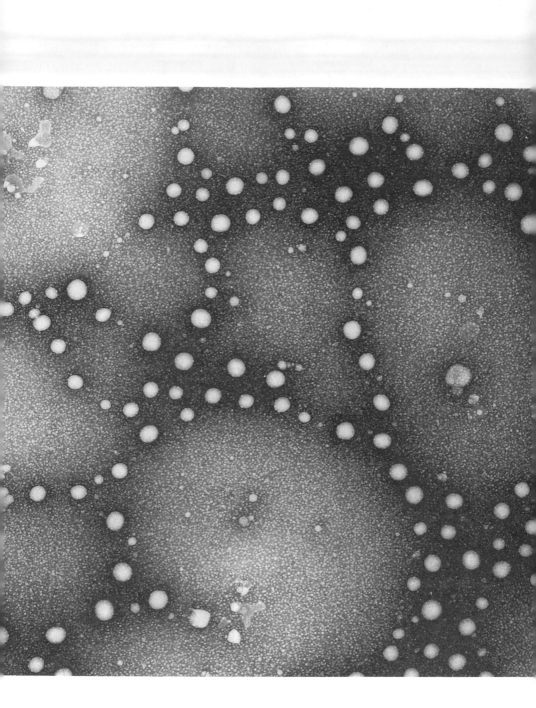

HDLs, the "good" lipoproteins

Higher levels of HDL, in the 70s and 80s, are thought to be protective against heart disease. Some scientists think that if the HDL level is below 35, the person is at risk of developing atherosclerosis even if his or her total cholesterol is in the safe zone.

As LDLs travel through the bloodstream, they are pulled into the cells by special protein receptors on the surface of the cells. Normally, the LDLs that are not caught by the receptors are carried to the liver, where they are converted into bile acid and eventually excreted by the body. But when too many fats are eaten, the bloodstream becomes flooded with tiny particles carrying fats and cholesterol out of the intestines to the rest of the body. The liver is so busy trying to get rid of these fatty particles that it can't handle the excess LDLs in the blood. These excess particles begin circulating freely throughout the body and can lead to the formation of plaque. The HDLs, on the other hand, travel through the bloodstream like empty envelopes, picking up the bits of excess cholesterol and carrying them back to the liver for processing.

TRIGLYCERIDES

Triglycerides consist of three fatty-acid molecules attached to one molecule of glycerol. These fatty acids can be saturated or unsaturated. Triglycerides make up approximately 95 percent of the fat and oil that we eat, as well as the fat traveling through our blood and stored in our body. Like cholesterol, a high level of triglycerides in the blood has been linked to coronary heart disease.

Studies show that triglyceride levels in the blood rise when sugar is consumed. This may happen because sugar causes the body to produce more insulin, which converts blood glucose into fatty acids and triglycerides. There is controversy over how much of a factor sugar is in the development of coronary heart disease. Some think that the rise in triglyceride levels caused by sugar is significant. Others, including a panel of blood-fat experts brought together by the National Institutes of Health, do not consider the temporary rise in triglycerides dangerous for most people. They feel that obesity, a high-fat diet, and a lack of exercise contribute more to heart disease than does too much sugar.

FATS IN THE DIET

Countless research has gone into finding which foods affect the level of serum cholesterol. The main goal has been to find foods that will lower the amount of LDLs in the blood while raising the HDLs. Much of that research has centered around fats.

The fats that we eat are classified as *saturated*, *monounsaturated*, and *polyunsaturated*. Saturated fats, the ones that are generally hard at room temperature, are the most likely to increase serum cholesterol. The liver uses saturated fat to make cholesterol, so the more saturated fat a food contains, the more it is likely to raise serum cholesterol.

Saturated fats are found in meats and in dairy products such as whole milk, butter, cream, and cheese. Some oils are high in saturated fats, too. Coconut oil contains the most saturated fat, followed closely by palm oil. Because of their long shelf life, these oils are frequently used in commercial products. Some of these products are advertised as being "cholesterol free," but this is misleading. Although they may not contain the cholesterol itself, they do contain the saturated fats that can raise the level of cholesterol in the body.

Polyunsaturated fats are soft or liquid at room temperature. All vegetable oils are cholesterol free and most are rich in polyunsaturated fat. The ones that are the least saturated are corn, cottonseed, soybean, sunflower, and safflower oils. Polyunsaturated fats tend to lower the level of cholesterol in the blood.

oils instead of olive

Until recently it was believed that monounsaturated fats, such as olive and peanut oil, were "neutral," neither raising nor lowering serum cholesterol levels. But more recent studies suggest that monounsaturates may be even better than polyunsaturates at reducing levels of harmful cholesterol. Although polyunsaturates reduce both HDLs and LDLs, the monounsaturates seem to remove mostly LDLs, or "bad" cholesterol, leaving the HDLs, or "good cholesterol," intact.

Meat is a good source of some nutrients,
but it is often high in saturated fats.
Try to choose lean cuts of meat
and avoid eating the fatty parts.

Some fats and oils are liquid in the beginning but are "hydrogenated" to make them solid. These fats are found mostly in shortening and margarine. Although these products are advertised as having no cholesterol, they are as harmful as saturated fats. Most commercially baked foods contain a high percentage of hydrogenated fat.

In recent years, another fat has been found to have cholesterol-lowering properties. Studies showed that the Eskimos of Greenland had low levels of serum cholesterol even though their diets were high in fat and cholesterol and low in carbohydrates. The secret ingredient in the Eskimo diet appears to be fish oil.

The fat in cold-water fish is polyunsaturated; this allows it to stay liquid even in very cold water. Fish oil also contains Omega-3 fatty acids, which are two to five times better than polyunsaturates at reducing serum cholesterol. These fatty acids also produce a substance that makes blood platelets less likely to stick together to form clots. Eating large quantities of fish oil has given the Eskimos a low risk of heart disease, but the studies also showed that they tend to bruise easily and have a harder time stopping bleeding when it occurs.

The best fish oils come from cold, deep-water ocean fish such as salmon, mackerel, tuna, and sardines, and from freshwater trout. Just two servings of these fish each week will generally provide enough Omega-3 fatty acids to slow down the formation of blood clots, but a very large intake of fish oil is necessary to lower serum cholesterol levels. Few people, other than Eskimos, are likely to eat this much fish oil.

Health food stores were quick to take advantage of these new findings, by selling fish-oil supplements, but until more research is available, most doctors and nutritionists are hesitant to recommend them. It would require fifteen to thirty capsules a day to duplicate the amount of fish oil consumed by the Eskimos. This is not only expensive but could be fattening. Also, the long-term effects of Omega-3 fatty acids are not known. The fish oil reduces the blood's ability to clot, and this may be dangerous in case of accident or injury. Instead of swallowing a handful of pills, it may make more sense to just add a few servings of fish to the diet each week.

LOWERING CHOLESTEROL

Some foods do seem to help lower the level of serum cholesterol. Soluble fibers, such as oat and rice bran, can help remove cholesterol from the body, possibly by binding with cholesterol and bile acids. Insoluble fibers, such as wheat or corn bran, do not affect blood cholesterol.

A nationwide rush for oat bran began after researchers found that eating 1 ½ to 3 ounces (42.5 to 85 g) of oat bran daily for six to eight weeks lowered the body's serum cholesterol level approximately 20 percent, and LDLs by as much as 25 percent. But many people have gone overboard in consuming oat products without paying attention to the other ingredients. These products often contain saturated fats, such as coconut oil, or are high in total fat and sugar. Some people think that eating oats allows them to safely eat fatty meats and other foods high in cholesterol. Reading product labels and using common sense must be part of any nutritional program.

Recent studies suggest that niacin, a common B vitamin, may help reduce cholesterol in the blood. However, it can cause side effects such as flushing and stomach disorders. Niacin supplements should only be taken when recommended by a physician.

Strangely enough, the best way to increase the amount of HDLs in the blood is not through diet but through exercise. A report published by the Centers for Disease Control stated that the lack of exercise is at least as dangerous to the heart as smoking a pack of cigarettes a day, having elevated blood cholesterol, or high blood pressure. Some figures show that a complete lack of physical activity increases the risk of death from heart disease by as much as 85 percent.

SMOKING AND HEART DISEASE

One factor that greatly increases the risk of heart disease is smoking. Although the exact reasons are not clear, experts suspect that smoking affects the heart in many ways. The nicotine found in cigarettes makes the heart beat faster and increases the cells' need for more oxygen. At the same time, the carbon monoxide constantly added to the bloodstream of smokers reduces the blood's ability to transport oxygen. It also appears that smoking causes the platelets to become stickier, allowing greater clumping of the blood. Substances entering the blood during smoking may damage the lining of the vessels in the heart, allowing cholesterol and other fatty substances to pass through the blood vessel wall. These factors speed the development of heart disease by injuring the artery lining as well as decreasing the blood's ability to carry oxygen to the heart muscle.

In women who take birth control pills, the risk of smoking is even greater. Research has found that combining smoking with taking the pill multiplies the risk of an early heart attack by forty times.

REDUCING THE RISKS
OF HEART DISEASE

The three best ways to reduce the risks of coronary heart disease are to quit smoking, start exercising, and improve the diet. Few people would disagree with the first two suggestions mentioned, but when it comes to diet, few people are in agreement about what should be done.

There is some controversy, for example, over whether everyone needs to alter his or her diet or just those at risk of developing heart disease. The American Heart Association recommends that all healthy Americans over the age of two limit their total fat intake to about 30 percent of their calories, with only 10 percent of those calories coming from saturated fats. It recommends limiting cholesterol intake to less than 300 milligrams per day.

On the other side, a report published in 1980 by the Food and Nutrition Board of the National Research Council, National Academy of Sciences, concluded that there was not enough convincing evidence to recommend that everyone reduce the amount of cholesterol he or she eats. The concern is that healthy people trying to cut down on fat and cholesterol may stop eating meat and eggs, which are excellent sources of high quality protein as well as zinc and iron. Eliminating these foods may make it difficult to meet the body's requirements for these nutrients.

It is still not totally clear what effect dietary cholesterol (the cholesterol you eat) has on serum cholesterol (the cholesterol in your blood). Most of the cholesterol in our blood is made by the body. The liver is able to increase or decrease the amount of cholesterol it makes depending on the amount in the diet. But heredity also plays a significant role in how the body handles cholesterol. Some individuals have an inherited defect, causing them to make too much cholesterol no matter how little they eat. Others are able to eat foods high in cholesterol and saturated fats and still maintain normal blood levels.

Many doctors think that those individuals with low levels of serum cholesterol do not necessarily need to restrict their cholesterol intake to the recommended 300 mg per day. However, those who have a family history of heart disease and other risk factors such as obesity, hypertension, or diabetes should watch their cholesterol levels and plan their diets accordingly.

Changes in diet and life-style seem to be working. The death rate from cardiovascular disease declined by 36 percent between 1963 and 1983. Part of this was due to better medical care. But as much as 60 percent of the reduction came from better health habits. More people are quitting smoking, exercising more, and changing their diets to lower the amount of fat and cholesterol they eat. Knowing your risks and taking steps to reduce them will go a long way in having a heart that will work properly for many, many years.

———THREE———

AVOIDING THE RISKS
OF CANCER

At least one out of every four Americans will develop some type of cancer during his or her lifetime. Cancer is the second leading cause of death in the United States. Although there are many different types of cancer affecting various parts of the body, all have one thing in common—a pattern of uncontrolled cell growth that eventually destroys healthy tissue.

A healthy body controls the rate at which its cells divide, so that just the right number of cells are created to replace the ones that have been lost. These normal cells stay within their natural boundaries. But cancer cells begin dividing wildly and spread into other parts of the body, invading organs such as the liver, brain, bone marrow, and so on. These spreading cells, called *tumors*, keep the organs they invade from functioning normally.

CAUSES OF CANCER

In order for a cancer to form, a susceptible host must be available as well as a cancer-causing substance called a *carcinogen*. There are several theories on how carcinogens work. One suggests that they damage the cell's genetic material, the DNA. The DNA, or deoxyribonucleic acid, is important in regulating the cell's division and also carries the cell's identity, which is passed on from one generation of cells to the next. If a carcinogen damages the DNA, it changes the cell's nature, and the damage is passed on to new cells. For this to happen, the carcinogen usually has to be present for a long time. Damage to the "daughter" cells comes when the cell divides, before the DNA has had a chance to repair itself.

There are two types of carcinogens involved in the development of cancer. Some, called *initiators*, actually change the DNA and begin the process of abnormal cell growth. Other carcinogens, called *promoters*, provide the damaged cells with a better chance of growing into a tumor.

We know that nutrition plays an important role in preventing and lessening the effects of cancer, but this connection is harder to study than the link between diet and heart disease. It may take cancer twenty or thirty years to develop to the point where it can be detected, making the exact cause difficult to pinpoint.

Although the link between diet and cancer is

still unclear, there is one area where the facts cannot be disputed. The major single cause of cancer deaths in the United States is cigarette smoking. This habit is responsible for about 30 percent of the deaths from cancer, more than all other known carcinogens added together.

THE EFFECTS OF
DIET ON CANCER

Next to avoiding tobacco in all forms, following a healthy diet is the most important factor in reducing cancer risks. An estimated 40 percent of all cancers in men and 60 percent of all cancers in women are caused by the foods they eat.

Of all the elements in the diet, fat is most closely related to the development of cancer. Hundreds of studies have linked a high fat diet with cancers of the breast, prostate, colon, liver, and pancreas. Breast cancer, the most common type of cancer for American women, is rarely found in women living in Japan. But if these Japanese women move to the United States and adopt our high fat diet, their incidence of breast cancer becomes equal to that of American women.

The second most common form of cancer for both men and women is cancer of the colon. This type of cancer is also linked to a diet high in fat and cholesterol and low in fiber. It should not come as any surprise that countries that have a high incidence of heart disease also have a great number of people with colon cancer. The same high-fat, low-fiber diet that is unhealthy for hearts is also likely to increase the risks of cancer.

Fat may not cause cancer (some studies have indicated it does), but it is at least a promotor of it, helping cancerous cells to multiply once they have formed. Although saturated fats are linked to the development of heart disease, it is the polyunsaturated fats that are more likely to promote cancer, and some studies have indicated they are a major source of *free radicals*.

Free radicals are highly reactive compounds produced during oxidation. Oxidation is the process in which food is burned in the presence of oxygen; this provides fuel for the body. Free radicals travel through the body like pyromaniacs, oxidizing and destroying tissue and creating more new free radicals. One of their most destructive actions is to damage the DNA within cells, causing changes that may eventually lead to cancer.

Although the body makes free radicals, it also is able to get rid of them with certain vitamins that act as antioxidants. These vitamins react with the free radicals and prevent their oxidation into potentially harmful substances. Vitamins A, C, and E are all antioxidants. Uric acid, which until recently was thought of only as a waste product, is also a potent antioxidant.

Although antioxidants, such as vitamin C, may help prevent cancer by blocking free radical activity, they can't help people who already have cancer. Researchers at the Mayo Clinic in Rochester, Minnesota, gave large doses of vitamin C to patients with advanced, incurable cancer. They found no significant difference in the death rate between patients who had taken the vitamin C and those who had not.

Food additives have long been suspected of causing cancer, but most of these claims are unsubstantiated. Even so, some food additives, such as Red Dye No. 2, have been banned in recent years because high doses were found to cause cancer in laboratory animals.

The link between cancer and nitrate preservatives has also been questioned. These chemicals have been used to cure meats for over two thousand years. Nitrates occur naturally in many plants and even in our own saliva. Only about 20 percent of our daily nitrate intake comes from additives found in such foods as bacon, hot dogs, and cold cuts; the rest comes from natural sources. In their natural state, nitrates are not harmful, but when they reach the stomach they are converted to compounds called nitrosamines, which have been found to cause cancer in test animals.

Nitrate has not been banned because it is needed to prevent the formation of spores that cause *botulism*, the most serious form of food poisoning. Adding nitrates to cured meats and other products allows them to be processed, transported, and stored without fear of an outbreak of botulism. Thus, the overall benefits of nitrate far outweigh its risks.

Harmful effects of nitrates in the stomach can

be blocked by antioxidants such as vitamin C—if they are taken at the same time. Food manufacturers are aware of this, and many of them have begun including vitamin C with the nitrates in order to prevent carcinogens from forming.

Certain foods can be carcinogenic if they contain *aflatoxins,* which are naturally occurring poisons produced by certain molds. Aflatoxins are found mostly in nuts, grains, and seeds. These foods should be kept in dry, sealed containers to discourage the growth of mold. Nuts, grains, and seeds that are sold commercially in the United States are monitored for safety and quality by the Food and Drug Administration (FDA) and by industry. Still, any of them that appear moldy should be thrown away.

The way we cook our food may also be linked to cancer formation. Fried foods can contribute to cancer in two ways. First, they add fat to the diet. But perhaps even more dangerous is that cooking at high heats may produce chemicals that have been shown to damage the DNA of bacteria in laboratory tests. Whenever possible, frying should be done with as little fat as possible and at lower temperatures, below 300° F (149° C).

Some people worry about charcoal-broiled meat. Picnickers have worried for years about the "burnt stuff" on their hamburgers, which may contain carcinogens. Although it is true that charring meat does create toxic compounds, most people eat too little smoked or charred meat in a lifetime to worry about it.

Also considered carcinogenic are some pesticides and other chemicals used in growing produce. In early 1989, a report by the Natural Resources Defense Council claimed that a chemical called daminozide, or Alar, sprayed mainly on apples, increased the risk of cancer in children. Risks were considered greater for children who eat more produce relative to their body weight and who may not metabolize toxins as efficiently as adults. Near panic followed the report as mothers poured apple juice down the drain and entire school districts stopped serving apples to their students. However, their reaction may have been extreme. At that time only 5 percent of the apples in the United States were being treated with Alar. Later, three federal agencies responsible for food safety declared that apples were not dangerous to eat and that Alar was not an "imminent hazard" to children. Still, the EPA has proposed a complete ban on Alar, to go into effect in 1990.

The publicity surrounding the Alar report raised suspicions about the safety of all fruits and vegetables. Although no one can guarantee that our food supply is 100 percent safe, it is among the safest in the world today. The EPA sets limits for the amounts of residue left in foods, limits that are well below what it considers to be danger levels. Eliminating fruits and vegetables from the diet in order to avoid pesticides would pose a greater health risk than the pesticides themselves. Exposure to pesticides can be reduced by careful washing of fruits and vegetables before eating them. It is also wise to buy domestic produce, because imports may contain more pesticides, some of which have been banned in the United States.

FOODS THAT PROTECT AGAINST CANCER

Although some foods increase the risks of developing cancer, there are some nutrients that offer partial protection from this disease. One such nutrient is fiber, that part of plant food that can't be digested. British physicians in Uganda found that colon cancer, as well as several other diseases, were rare in that country. They believed that the low cancer rate was due to the African diet, which consists mostly of grains and high-fiber foods with very little fat.

There are two types of fibers, those that are soluble in water and those that aren't. The soluble fibers, such as rice and oat bran, are beneficial in reducing the amount of cholesterol in the blood, thus reducing the risk of heart disease. The insoluble fibers, such as wheat and corn bran, are more beneficial in reducing cancer risk.

Insoluble fibers act like sponges to absorb water. They tend to move food quickly through the stomach and intestines, taking up water along the way and thus making stools larger and softer. The water held by these fibers may dilute chemicals in the feces that could have a damaging effect on the cells of the intestinal wall. Fiber may also help move dangerous chemicals out of the intestine more quickly, before they can do much harm.

Bran cereals have become the latest rage because they are high in fiber and, by themselves, low in fat. Be careful, however, to choose products with bran that don't add fatty or sugary ingredients to improve the flavor.

Including more fruits, vegetables, and whole grains in the diet makes sense, but taking commercial fiber supplements does not. Excessive amounts of fiber can lead to some uncomfortable side effects such as gas, bloating, and diarrhea. Large amounts of fiber can block the absorption of calcium, magnesium, iron, and zinc. Increasing fiber in the diet should be done gradually.

Several vitamins and minerals are also believed to offer some protection from cancer. As mentioned before, vitamins A, C, and E are known to be strong antioxidants and thus protect cells from free radicals. Another substance that has received much publicity lately is beta-carotene, which is converted by the body into vitamin A. Beta-carotene is found in dark green, deep yellow, and orange vegetables. Studies over a long period of time found that men who rarely ate foods containing beta-carotene were eight times more likely to develop lung cancer than those who regularly ate foods high in that nutrient.

Another group of beneficial vegetables are those in the cabbage family. Called cruciferous vegetables because they have four-petaled flowers that form a crucifer, or cross, these vegetables, including cabbage, broccoli, cauliflower, Brussels sprouts, and mustard greens, are believed to contain a chemical that stimulates the liver's production of enzymes. In turn, these enzymes can inactivate certain toxic chemicals.

There may also be some minerals that can help prevent certain types of cancer. It is now believed that calcium and vitamin D offer some protection from colon cancer. Some studies have shown that men who drink milk have a lower risk of colon cancer than those who don't. Many doctors believe that for those with a family history of colon cancer, calcium supplements may reverse a dangerous pattern of cell growth in the lining of the colon, a pattern that often precedes cancer.

Recently, more interest has been taken in the trace element selenium as an antioxidant. Scientists wanted to know if the high rate of breast and colon cancer in New Zealand had anything to do with the low levels of selenium in their soil. Research done in the United States and other countries has supported this theory, showing that diets rich in selenium reduce the chance of developing several types of cancer. However, selenium supplements should not be taken without a doctor's supervision because the toxic level of a dose is so low that supplements could prove dangerous. Most people get all the selenium they need from seafood, wheat germ, and whole grains.

MAKING CHANGES

It is now believed that environmental factors, such as smoking, diet, and exposure to hazardous chemicals and radiation cause as much as 90 percent of the cancers in the United States. Since most of these elements can be controlled to some extent, cancer is potentially a preventable disease. Next to a commitment not to smoke, changing the diet appears to be the most effective way to improve your chances of avoiding various types of cancer.

In making dietary changes, it isn't necessary to give up all the foods you like in order to reduce your cancer risk. But in making food choices, choose *more often* those foods that may reduce your risk of cancer. These include high-fiber foods such as fruits, grains, and vegetables, as well as foods rich in vitamin A, vitamin C, and beta-carotene. Choose *less often* those foods that may increase your cancer risk, including foods high in fats of all kinds, and smoked, salt-cured, and pickled foods. Your food choices should depend on the foods you like, your weight and height, and how close your current eating habits are to recommended diets.

FOUR

DIETARY TREATMENT OF DISEASE

OSTEOPOROSIS

Each year over 300,000 women in the United States fracture their hips. Some 10 to 15 percent die within six months of complications resulting from the fracture, while only about one-third of the rest ever return to a normal, rehabilitated life. These fractures are caused by the disease osteoporosis, or "porous bones."

Osteoporosis afflicts mostly older women and is caused by the deterioration of bone over time. These bones may become so weak that they crack under the body weight they are carrying. Often, the spinal column begins to collapse, reducing the woman's height and producing the back deformity known as a "widow's hump."

Bones are living tissue and are constantly being rebuilt and replaced. In addition to acting as the body's framework, bones serve as storehouses

for calcium. When there is not enough calcium in the blood to do all the mineral's important jobs, such as regulating fluid levels, transmitting nerve impulses, and powering muscle contractions, the body takes the calcium it needs from the bones. The more calcium taken, the thinner the bones become. Eventually, the bones become so thin that they fracture easily.

Bone loss increases after menopause, when menstruation ceases permanently. At this time, women's estrogen levels fall sharply. Since estrogen blocks the hormones that remove calcium from the bones, the loss of this hormone accelerates bone loss. This happens even in certain groups of younger women, such as long-distance runners, gymnasts, dancers, and women who have anorexia nervosa. Such women have very little body fat, low levels of estrogen, and irregular or nonexistent menstrual periods. By losing bone mass at a time when they should be building it up, these women are likely to have even more serious problems when they are older.

Some women are at greater risk of developing osteoporosis than others. Black women have greater bone density than white women, so are

Osteoporosis, or bone loss, is the cause of the "widow's hump," seen most often in elderly women.

less likely to have problems. Small-boned, fair-skinned women of northern European descent are the most vulnerable.

The good news about osteoporosis is that it is basically a preventable disease. Women can reduce their risks by building up as much bone mass as possible while they are young, and by keeping bone loss to a minimum when they are older.

Building and maintaining strong bones involves a combination of diet and exercise. The most important mineral, but not the only one, needed to build and maintain bone is calcium. Adults need 800 milligrams of calcium each day. That is equivalent to three cups of milk or 4 ounces (113 g) of cheese daily. Higher amounts, between 1,200 and 1,500 milligrams daily, are recommended for adolescents and women who are pregnant or nursing babies.

Eating enough calcium doesn't guarantee that the body will get all it needs. Calcium can get tangled up with other nutrients in the digestive tract and never make it into the bloodstream. Although fiber is good for many things, it can bind with calcium and keep the calcium from being absorbed. Large amounts of protein, salt, and caffeine have also been shown to increase the amount of calcium excreted in the urine. Even phosphorus, which is also needed for bone growth, can hinder calcium absorption if too much is taken. This may create a problem for people who take in more phosphorus than they do calcium, such as those who avoid milk but drink a lot of phosphate-containing diet sodas.

Those who cannot get enough calcium through diet alone can take calcium supplements. Calcium carbonate tablets provide calcium in its most usable form. Many antacids contain this type of calcium, but users should read the labels to be sure of what they are getting. Some foods, such as cereals, flour, and orange juice, now contain extra calcium for those who have trouble getting it elsewhere.

Adding fluoride to drinking water has long been shown to reduce the incidence of tooth decay. More recently, evidence has suggested that it may also protect against osteoporosis. Research has shown that communities with a higher concentration of fluoride in their water have fewer cases of osteoporosis than communities whose water has little or no fluoride. For these reasons, many communities add this mineral to their water when normal levels are low. Unfortunately, in spite of fluoride's known benefits and safety, some groups are still afraid of it and are adamantly opposed to adding it to their water.

Another necessary element in the prevention of osteoporosis is exercise. Weight-bearing exercises, such as walking, jogging, tennis, and so on, put physical stress on the bones. The body responds by increasing bone density. Exercise also increases the flow of blood to the bones, making bone-building nutrients more available. But just as

exercise builds bones, a lack of exercise can weaken them. This is especially true in women who, for one reason or another, have been confined to bed or to a wheelchair for long periods of time. Even living a sedentary life will increase the risk of osteoporosis.

Since a loss of estrogen is a factor in bone loss, estrogen replacement therapy is becoming widely recommended for women who have reached menopause. In the past, doctors were reluctant to prescribe estrogen because of its possible link to cancer. But today's estrogen doses contain only 10 percent of the original strength and are balanced with a second hormone, progesterone. These doses are considered safe for most women. Estrogen skin patches are now available that release estrogen straight into the bloodstream without having to go through the liver. This means that lower doses can be used to get the same benefits.

Weight lifting is effective for building and strengthening bone, but it shouldn't be done by people with certain chronic diseases, such as hypertension, or by young people still growing.

HYPERTENSION

Hypertension, or high blood pressure, is a problem for more than 60 million Americans. It has been called the silent killer because it usually has no obvious symptoms. Yet hypertension contributes to about 500,000 strokes every year and is a major risk factor in heart attacks and kidney disease.

Blood pressure is the force of blood pushing against artery walls as it is being pumped through the body. Two numbers are given in blood pressure readings. When blood pressure is 120/80, the first number shows the maximum pressure (systolic), which is measured when the heart contracts to pump blood. The lower number is the minimum (diastolic) pressure that is measured when the heart rests between beats. Physicians generally consider anything above 140/90 to be too high.

Stress, excitement, anxiety, and physical activity can temporarily raise the blood pressure. Having just one high reading is not considered hypertension. But when the blood pressure is consistently high, it must be treated to avoid permanent damage.

Hypertension is dangerous for many reasons. It increases the risk of heart disease by forcing the heart to work harder. It may promote atherosclerosis by injuring the lining of the artery and thus increasing the buildup of plaque. It can cause strokes either by rupturing the brain's fragile blood vessels or by creating clots that block the flow of blood to the brain. Hypertension can also damage the kidneys.

The exact cause of hypertension is not yet known, but it is most likely a combination of heredity and environment. We know that it is more common in men than in women (except those women taking oral contraceptives). It is more likely to be found in people who are black, over sixty-five, overweight, or have a family history of the disease. Personality type may also be a factor. Some studies indicate that people with high blood pressure tend to be irritable, tense, anxious, and restless.

Some groups, including the Federal Drug Administration and the American Medical Association, suggest that consuming too much sodium, mainly in the form of salt, is a major contributor to hypertension. They theorize that since sodium encourages the body to retain fluids, it could increase the blood volume, resulting in a rise in blood pressure. This theory has gotten some support from experiments where feeding salt to laboratory animals has resulted in higher blood pressure. However, its effect on humans is not as clear.

It hasn't been proven that excess salt is bad for most of the population. Studies have shown that only one third to one half of people with hypertension are sensitive to sodium. For most of the population, sodium seems to have little effect on blood pressure. However, those who already have hypertension should limit their salt intake to see if this improves the condition. Although cutting back on salt may not be necessary, it certainly won't hurt anyone to do so. The average American diet includes ten to thirty-five times the amount of salt needed by the body.

Recent studies have led doctors to believe that calcium—not sodium—may have more influence on hypertension in some people. In 1984 researchers at Oregon Health Sciences University studied data on more than 10,000 people to see how the intake of seventeen different nutrients related to blood pressure. No evidence was found linking sodium to hypertension. But researchers found that people with hypertension consistently had a lower calcium intake than normal. Some patients were able to lower their blood pressure significantly by adding a gram of calcium to their daily diets for eight weeks. Others saw no improvement with calcium. The Oregon study also found that hypertensives were likely to lack adequate levels of potassium as well.

Weight loss will successfully lower blood pressure, especially in patients who are more than 15 percent above their ideal weight. Excess weight raises blood pressure both by increasing blood volume and by requiring the heart to pump harder. Even a slight weight loss helps, perhaps because dieting tends to slow the body's metabolism, which may make the heart pump more slowly and result in a drop of blood pressure.

Drugs can be used to treat hypertension, but doctors are more likely to try dietary and lifestyle changes first because of the possible side effects of medication. Besides the possibility of suffering from gout, fatigue, and impotence, there is some indication that the medication used to treat hypertension also raises the levels of fat in the blood. Doctors prefer to control the hypertension without medication, or at least give a reduced dosage.

Dietary changes usually include reducing sodium intake, but this is not easy to achieve. Only about a third of the salt we eat comes from the saltshaker. Another third occurs naturally in food, and the rest is added during food processing. High levels of sodium can also be present in drinking water, especially when it has been softened by a commercial water softener.

Exercise is also helpful in lowering blood pressure because it helps reduce weight and stress. Exercise improves circulation and helps the heart to function more efficiently. However, strengthening exercises, such as weight lifting, can give blood pressure a short but intense boost and do hypertensives more harm than good. Moderate aerobic exercises are best.

Blood pressure should be checked once or twice a year so that hypertension can be detected and treated early, before the disease has had a chance to do any permanent damage to the body.

DIABETES MELLITUS

Diabetes mellitus is a disease in which an insufficient amount of insulin is produced by the body. Insulin is a hormone that allows tissues to take up glucose from the blood for use as fuel or to store as fat for future use. Diabetics have high levels of glucose in the blood but low levels in the tissues, where it is needed. If diabetes is allowed to go untreated, it can result in atherosclerosis, heart attack, stroke, gangrene of the extremities, kidney disease, and blindness.

There are two types of diabetes mellitus. The most serious is insulin-dependent diabetes, also called juvenile-onset because it appears early in life. In this type, insulin-producing cells in the pancreas have been destroyed by a virus or by genetic or environmental factors. As a result, little or no insulin is made, blood sugar rises, and the tissues are starved for fuel. This type of diabetes is inherited and is not caused by eating too much sugar, as some people think.

Treatment for insulin-dependent diabetes includes daily doses of insulin, usually given as shots or through an implanted pump that automatically delivers the insulin to the bloodstream. In addition to insulin, the treatment must include a carefully balanced diet.

The more common type of diabetes mellitus is non-insulin-dependent, also referred to as adult-onset. Here, the pancreas still makes the needed insulin, but the body's cells can't make proper use of the hormone. This disease normally strikes overweight men and women past age forty who have a family history of diabetes.

Unlike the first type, adult-onset diabetes can be prevented somewhat, through weight control.

Diabetics are often obese. Their excessive fat tissue increases the body's resistance to the action of insulin. This type of diabetes can usually be controlled by diet and exercise alone, although insulin may occasionally be required. It has been found that diabetics don't have to lose as much weight as previously thought in order to control the disease. However, the weight must be lost in the early stages of the disease and kept off permanently.

Scientists and doctors still don't know exactly what causes diabetes, but they are learning what *doesn't* cause it. They know that eating sugar will not, by itself, bring on diabetes. And although obesity usually goes along with diabetes, obesity alone won't cause the disease. Genetics appear to be the primary cause.

Although diet may not cause diabetes, it is very important in the treatment of the disease. Over the years the type of diet recommended for diabetics has changed. Before insulin was available, doctors controlled the disease by keeping the patient's carbohydrate level so low that little glucose was able to build up in the bloodstream. Then researchers found that high-fiber meals lowered blood sugar more than low-fiber meals did. Now doctors realize that diabetics don't necessarily need *low* levels of glucose in their blood as much as they need relatively *even* levels. Today, the complex carbohydrates and fiber that were once discouraged are recommended because they release glucose into the bloodstream more gradually.

To keep blood glucose at an even level,

insulin-dependent diabetics need to be consistent in their eating habits. Each meal should contain approximately the same proportion of protein, fat, and carbohydrate and the same number of calories as every other meal. Planning meals for diabetics used to be complicated until the Exchange Lists were developed. The Exchange Lists group similar foods together. Each item within a list contains about the same amount of carbohydrate, protein, fat, and calories. By choosing the recommended number of items from each list, a balanced meal can be put together.

A newer tool that may someday aid diabetics in choosing their foods is the Glycemic Index, which ranks different foods as to how quickly they raise blood glucose. Formulating the Glycemic Index produced some surprising results. For example, ice cream releases glucose into the bloodstream more gradually than potatoes do. With the Glycemic Index as a guide, diabetics in the future may be able to measure their own responses to various foods and work out individualized diets. However, more research is needed to see if a standardized index is feasible for people with diabetes.

Because they often have high levels of fats in the blood, which increase the risk of heart disease, diabetics need to limit the amount of fat in their diet. They must also avoid simple sugars since these are absorbed very rapidly and will raise blood sugar to very high levels.

Doctors have changed their thinking on the role of exercise in diabetes. They used to think that sports would overtax young people with diabetes, but now they know that exercise has benefits. It not only helps control weight and burns up excess glucose in the blood, it can make the cells more receptive to insulin. However, any person with diabetes engaging in sports or vigorous exercise needs to first learn how to control his or her glucose level.

IRON-DEFICIENCY ANEMIA

Iron is one of the most abundant minerals in the earth's crust, yet iron deficiency is one of the world's most common nutritional problems. Iron is present in every cell in the body, but most of it is found in the blood as part of hemoglobin, the substance in red blood cells responsible for carrying oxygen.

When red blood cells are broken down, the iron is reused to form new cells. Ordinarily, only about one milligram of iron a day is lost through urine, sweat, and sloughed-off skin. The adult male who has a good store of iron rarely becomes iron deficient. But females of childbearing age lose iron every month during menstruation. This iron must be replaced in the diet to avoid an iron deficiency.

When the body's reserves of iron are exhausted, production of hemoglobin begins to decline, resulting in iron-deficiency anemia. Without enough hemoglobin to equip new red cells properly, those cells are smaller and paler than normal.

They are not able to carry as much oxygen to the muscles and organs. The result is loss of energy and appetite, weakness and fatigue, shortness of breath, and a rapid heartbeat.

Iron deficiency affects both physical and intellectual productivity. Studies have shown that children don't learn as quickly when an iron deficiency is present, partly because of the lowered hemoglobin and partly because the lack of iron makes it difficult to resupply neurotransmitters in the brain.

During certain periods of life, the body's need for iron is greater, and deficiencies are more likely to occur. Infants use up their iron stores within the first six months and are often fed only milk, which is a poor source of iron. During periods of rapid growth, children and adolescents need more iron to keep up with their expanding blood volume and iron stores. Adolescent girls and women of childbearing years need more iron to replace menstrual losses. During pregnancy, a woman's iron needs can increase by more than 300 percent in order to meet the needs of her own expanding blood volume and tissues as well as the needs of the developing fetus.

Getting enough iron through diet alone can be a problem for some people because only about 10 percent of the iron taken in is actually absorbed. Red meat (especially organ meats such as liver), fish, and poultry are the best sources of iron because they provide heme iron, the form that is most readily absorbed by the body. Green leafy vegetables, such as spinach, are also good sources of iron.

In ancient times, physicians had their patients drink water that an iron sword had been dipped into so that they could absorb the strength of the sword. Today, many smart cooks use the same principle by cooking in iron pots and pans. During cooking the iron is leached from the pot into the food, especially if the food is acidic. For example, the iron content of 100 grams of spaghetti sauce simmered in a glass dish is 3 milligrams, but it becomes 87 milligrams when the same amount of sauce is cooked in an iron pot.

The absorption of iron is affected also by the other foods being eaten. Food containing 25 milligrams or more of vitamin C can more than double the amount of iron absorbed during a meal. Meat is not only a good source of iron in itself, it also aids in the absorption of iron from less satisfactory sources, such as vegetables.

Certain other foods can reduce the absorption of iron. A diet very high in fiber will move food through the intestines quickly, so that a smaller amount of iron will be absorbed. Also, the phytic acid present in cereals and grains can bind with iron and keep it from being absorbed as well. The tannins in tea also inhibit iron absorption, and, to a lesser extent, so will coffee. Since the stomach needs acid in order to work properly, using antacids reduces the amount of iron absorbed. This is why ulcer patients are at risk of developing iron-deficiency anemia.

Iron supplements, in the form of ferrous sulfate, may be recommended for those who cannot meet their need through diet alone. However, it must be remembered that taking an excess of one mineral can block the absorption of others. For instance, supplements containing only iron should not be taken at mealtime, when a heavy dose of iron is likely to inhibit the absorption of zinc. If a supplement is taken during a meal, it should be a balanced multimineral formula that will provide extra zinc as well as extra iron.

PEPTIC ULCERS

Peptic ulcers are caused by excessive gastric juices that wear away the lining of the stomach and the duodenum, the pouch at the entrance to the small intestine. This increase in gastric juices can be caused by a number of things, including tension or anxiety, alcohol, coffee (even the decaffeinated varieties), smoking, and a variety of different drugs, including aspirin. Eating habits may also contribute to the problem. Grabbing quick meals and gobbling them down means food is chewed poorly and the stomach must work harder to break it up.

The diets prescribed for ulcer patients has changed over the years. Bland diets containing a lot of milk and cream, sometimes as much as 3 ounces (85 ml) each hour, were once thought to be the best diet for ulcer patients. Doctors believed that these foods would coat the stomach, allowing the ulcer to heal. Anything highly seasoned was

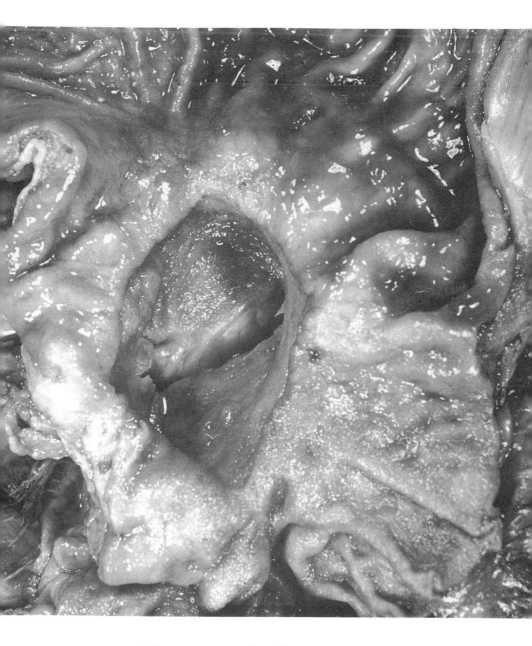

A human stomach with a peptic ulcer

forbidden. Not only were these diets high in fat and cholesterol, it has since been found that the dairy products stimulated the production of stomach acid, thus actually aggravating the ulcer more than healing it.

Today, ulcer patients can eat a fairly normal diet, which is much better for their mental outlook as well as their nutritional well-being. Some doctors may recommend antacids along with the avoidance of certain foods and alcohol, nicotine, coffee, aspirin, and arthritis drugs. Other doctors recommend eating several smaller meals throughout the day. Stress management is an important part of the treatment for those whose ulcers were caused by too much tension. Drugs are also prescribed when necessary.

There has been a recent decline in the number of stomach ulcer patients. Some researchers suggest that this is a result of the increased use of vegetable oils instead of animal fats. Studies have shown that linoleic acid, which is a component of vegetable oil, produces a hormonelike compound that may prevent stomach ulcers.

─────FIVE─────

WEIGHT CONTROL

In spite of America's obsession with fitness and thinness, our number one nutritional problem is obesity. An estimated 34 million adults in the United States are obese, meaning that they are more than 20 percent over desirable body weight due to excess body fat. Twelve million are considered morbidly obese, at least 100 pounds (45 kg) overweight or twice their recommended weight. The adjective "morbidly" is used to show that these individuals are in great danger of dying from heart disease, cancer, diabetes, or hypertension. Even Americans who are not obese are likely to weigh 15 to 30 pounds (6 to 14 kg) more than they should. It's no wonder so many people are concerned with weight control.

THE FAT-CELL THEORY

The "fat-cell theory" is one explanation of obesity. Scientists have found that many obese people have

more fat cells than thin people. In adults, the number of fat cells doesn't change; only the size of the cell does. Like little balloons, these cells can expand to hold more fat when needed and shrink when some of the fat is removed.

Those with mild or moderate obesity, which usually develops in middle age, are thought to have a normal number of fat cells containing too much fat. Through diet and exercise, these people can shrink those fat cells down to their normal size. But those whose obesity began in childhood or adolescence probably have too many fat cells, each containing a normal amount of fat. In order to become thin, these people must reduce the size of those cells below normal, something the body is reluctant to do. As a result, people with too many fat cells have trouble reducing past a certain point no matter how hard they try. These empty fat cells may even cause an individual to eat more. Some researchers suggest that when fat cells get too empty they send chemical "hunger" signals to the brain.

Until recently, it was widely believed that fat cells formed through overeating, but only during critical periods, mainly infancy and adolescence. It

Obesity occurs in an estimated 34 million adults in the United States.

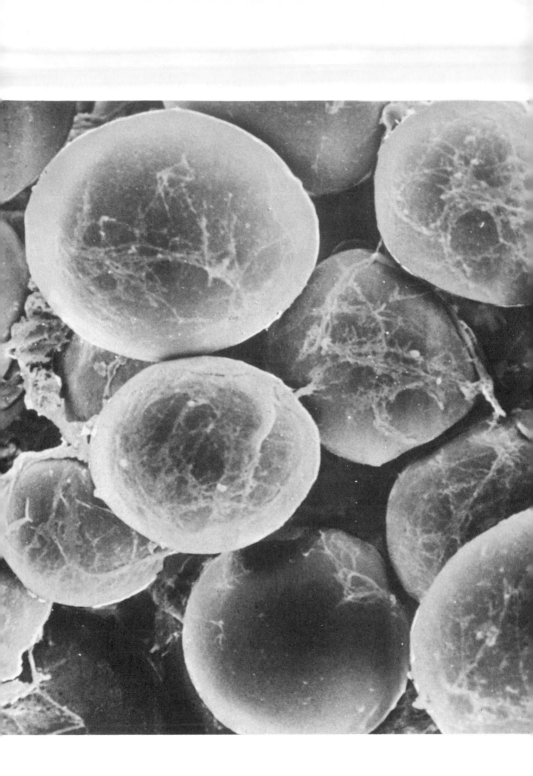

was believed that fat babies were destined to become fat adults. But this theory was based on experiments done with rats. Humans appear to react differently.

Today, many scientists have revised their thinking on fat cells. Most believe that infants don't add new fat cells their first year of life; they just fill up the ones they were born with. Fat cells are most likely to increase in number during the child's second year and again during adolescence, although they can be added at any point up to adulthood. This means that chubby babies don't necessarily grow up to be chubby adults. However, the more baby fat they have, and the longer they keep it, the harder it will be to take the fat off.

In some children with a strong genetic tendency toward obesity, fat cells may begin to increase in number even in the first year. Some children have as many fat cells as adults when they are only a few years old. However, unless a baby is obese, parents should not try to restrict his or her diet before the age of two. This would make it too difficult for the babies to get the nutrients they need to develop properly. Some parents think they are doing their babies a favor by feeding them skim milk and low-fat diets, but babies need more fat in their diets than older children or adults. They need

Fat cells magnified
110 times

the extra calories and the fat for the normal development of their nervous system.

The tendency toward obesity is inherited. Studies have shown that when one parent is obese, an individual has a 40 percent chance of becoming obese. That risk increases to 80 percent when both parents are obese. Only 10 percent of children born to lean parents have this problem. Genetics may contribute to obesity by dictating a high number of fat cells, a low metabolic rate, or both. (Metabolic rate refers to the number of calories the body uses to take care of its basic needs, such as breathing, heartbeat, tissue repair, body temperature, and so on.)

The genetic link to obesity can be seen in studies of adoptees. Children who are adopted are more likely to have the same type of weight as their birth parents instead of the adoptive parents who fed them. Also, identical twins separated at birth are similar in weight even when raised by two separate families with different eating patterns.

Although genes set the basic parameters on how fat or how thin a person can be, everyone still has a certain range of freedom to choose how they will look. Those who have a higher risk of obesity can lower their chances of being overweight with a lifelong commitment to good eating habits and regular exercise.

SETPOINT THEORY

Most individuals maintain a stable body weight over long periods of time. This has led some to

This family, owners of a concrete company, clearly share the genetic tendency toward obesity. Although obesity can be inherited, a proper diet and an active life-style can usually keep it in check.

believe in the setpoint theory, which suggests that the body has a certain weight that it will try to maintain no matter how many calories—within limits—are taken in. Your setpoint is the weight at which you stabilize when you make no special effort to gain or lose. It appears that when you drop below this point, chemical signals of starvation kick in, making you eat more until the weight is back to "normal," even though that weight may be higher than you want it to be.

The setpoint theory would explain why weight is regained so easily after a diet and why it is as difficult for thin people to gain weight as it is for fat people to lose it. However, evidence suggests that the weight-stabilizing mechanism only works properly for people who are reasonably active. Exercise can safely and permanently lower the setpoint, allowing the body to settle comfortably at a lower weight level. However, the setpoint will return to normal once the person stops exercising regularly.

ADDING POUNDS

Those who are not obese but merely overweight have their own reasons for adding extra pounds. For many, extra pounds begin to accumulate in midlife, when eating patterns remain the same in spite of a slowdown in activity.

Accumulating excess weight may be caused more by underactivity than by overeating. The control of hunger and appetite usually works quite well in active people and only fails when activity falls below a certain level. Researchers who have closely observed obese people have found that many of them eat less than lean people, but they are sometimes so extremely inactive that they still manage to have a surplus of calories.

For many families, the most fattening appliance in the home is the television. It encourages a sedentary life-style, increased snacking, and develops a desire for fattening foods through its commercials. At Tufts University, pediatrician William Dietz found a strong correlation between excessive TV watching and obesity. His studies determined that the amount of time a child aged six to eleven spent watching television was the best predictor of adolescent obesity. This is significant since obese adolescents usually become obese adults.

WEIGHT-LOSS DIETS

Yo-yo Dieting

A dangerous pattern develops among most overweight people. They go on a diet, lose weight, then quickly gain it all back. Frustrated with their failure, they go on another diet, lose more weight, then gain it back again. This pattern is repeated over and over again. The statistics are grim. Between 80 and 95 percent of the people who lose weight on diets will gain it back. The cycle of losing and gaining weight, called "yo-yo dieting," in most cases is more harmful than staying somewhat overweight.

"Quiet—I'm watching my workout tape!"

During dieting, while you are consuming fewer calories, your body adapts by lowering its metabolic rate so that it can get by on less. But when your old eating habits are resumed (the same habits that made you fat in the first place), your body is still existing on fewer calories. As a result, the lost pounds return.

Getting into a pattern of yo-yo dieting can eventually destroy the body's weight-regulation system. Some studies indicate that repeated dieting can train your body to reduce its basal metabolic rate more rapidly with each diet. With each succeeding diet you lose weight more slowly and regain it more quickly.

One startling discovery is that yo-yo dieting may actually make you fatter in the long run because it changes the body's actual composition. The pounds you lose are not the same pounds you gain back. Strict dieting makes you lose much of your lean muscle tissue. But when you put weight back on, it is usually in the form of fat. Since muscle tissue burns calories and fat tissue doesn't, it's senseless to get rid of the type of tissue that can keep you lean and replace it with the kind of tissue that will only make you fatter.

Repeated dieting not only increases the amount of fat in the body, it can also shift that fat to more undesirable areas. Research has shown that where fat is located on your body is important. Fat that is centered around the hips and thighs, as is usually the case with women, is less harmful than fat that accumulates around the abdomen. Abdominal fat is believed to increase the risks of heart disease and stroke.

Fad Diets

Because of their desperation to be thin, those who are overweight are quick to try any fad diet that sounds plausible. The only good thing about fad diets is that they are usually so restrictive that healthy people will not stay on one long enough to do any permanent nutritional damage to themselves. However, health problems are more common in those people who are chronic dieters and in those who rigidly follow extremely restricted diets.

Diets promising quick weight loss are the most popular. Although these diets may actually take off the weight they promise, they take off the *wrong kind* of weight. Scientists have shown that the faster you lose weight, the more water and muscle you are losing—and the less fat. So losing weight quickly only means that you are burning lean tissue rather than the fat you are trying to lose. The weight that is lost in the form of water quickly returns with normal eating.

Low-carbohydrate Diets

Diets low in carbohydrates have been popular because of the rapid loss of pounds the first week. However, since the weight loss is made up mostly of water, it is only temporary.

Cutting back on carbohydrates in order to lose weight doesn't make sense. Carbohydrates are the main source of energy for the body because they can most easily be turned into glucose, the body's fuel. Although fats can be used for energy by some parts of the body, other parts, such as the brain, can only use glucose.

When fat is burned without carbohydrates, the fat is only partially broken down. This forms dangerous toxic acids called ketones, which can put an extra strain on the kidneys. Water is used to flush these ketones out of the body, and it is this loss of water that is responsible for much of the early weight loss.

Carbohydrates spare the body's proteins so that they can be used for growth and tissue repair, instead of being used as an inefficient form of energy. If there aren't enough carbohydrates in the diet to make glucose, the body must turn to its stores of protein, found in the muscles, to make this substance. In a sense, the body is "eating itself" by destroying its muscle tissue to make glucose. People on low-carbohydrate diets may experience headaches, weakness, fatigue, and dizziness. Most people feel tired after only two days on the diet.

Another disadvantage of low-carbohydrate diets is that they are usually high in fat. Ounce for ounce, carbohydrates have only half as many calories as fats do, so more food can be eaten for the same number of calories.

Fasting and
Very Low-calorie Diets

Fasting is another unwise way to lose weight. It deprives the body of all, or nearly all, of its nourishment. It may seem like a quick way to get rid of unwanted pounds, but it is not the answer to permanent weight loss. It can lead to severe loss of muscle and fluids, as well as cause nutritional deficiencies.

Fasting may actually make your body fatter. When the body is cut off from food, it tries to make extra fat to get through the emergency. Skipping breakfast and lunch and only eating dinner will have the same effect, since the body sees that as a twenty-three-hour fast. It has also been shown that people who skip meals eat as much or more in that one meal as they would have by eating several smaller meals spread throughout the day.

Some liquid-protein diets, also called very low-calorie diets, generally provide between 400 and 800 calories a day. These diets were originally designed for the very obese, but some business people trying to make quick money came out with their own versions for the moderately overweight. The early liquid-protein diets used a poor protein

Carbohydrates are usually good sources of dietary fiber as well as glucose.

source, which led to several deaths from cardiac arrest. Today, the formulas are improved, but they still should only be used for those who are severely obese and only under the guidance of a physician, not just someone in a white coat who looks official.

Liquid-protein diets should not be confused with the commercial formula diets, such as Sego, that are sold in many grocery and drug stores. These formula diets evolved from infant formulas and supposedly include all the elements needed in a healthy diet. Although these diets generally won't do any harm, they don't teach the dieter anything about good eating habits. They can successfully take off weight in those who stick with them, but follow-up studies show that most dieters return to their original weight when they resume eating normally.

Like other rapid weight-loss schemes, low-calorie liquid diets lead to rapid weight gain as soon as the diet is over. This may be caused by a reduction in the metabolic rate and a tendency toward binge eating in those who have given up food for a long period of time. However, there are some strategies that may help dieters maintain their new lower weight. Behavior modification may help in breaking the bad habits that led to obesity in the first place. Being responsible to someone is also helpful, whether it is to a physician that helped in the weight loss or one of the many diet support groups. The most important element, however, in maintaining weight is exercise. In followup studies done on people who had lost weight, the number one predictor of success in keeping weight off was increased physical activity.

Novelty Diets

Also popular are so-called "novelty" diets that are based on unproven and sometimes bizarre information. These may emphasize one food group or drastically limit some elements in the diet such as fats or carbohydrates. They may have some magical combinations of foods that will supposedly burn off fat. One example is grapefruit, which promoters claim contains a special enzyme that will burn fat. Although grapefruit is a good low-calorie food, it doesn't have any magical qualities. In fact, scientists have not been able to find any food that has the ability to burn body fat.

An example of one diet where food is restricted is the Zen Macrobiotic diet. This diet is based on the notion that brown rice contains healing qualities. Unfortunately, brown rice not only lacks magical qualities, a diet emphasizing brown rice and little else does not provide the nutrients needed to sustain life. The most extreme version of this diet consists solely of brown rice and is dangerously deficient in essential nutrients. People have been known to starve to death on this diet.

Anti-cellulite Diet

Some people believe that cellulite (cell-u-LEET), the bumpy, dimply fat that often appears around the hips and thighs, is a distinct type of fat. They claim that it is made up of fat, water, and toxic wastes the body has failed to eliminate. Some suggest that getting rid of cellulite requires special diets, massage, exercise, and a number of other expensive treatments. Despite these claims, scientists have yet to discover any difference between cellulite and other forms of fat. Getting rid of cellulite requires a sensible diet and an exercise plan, preferably before age thirty-five to forty, while the skin is still elastic enough to shrink once the amount of fat has been reduced.

DIET DRUGS

It's hard to find a drug store, grocery store, or health food store that doesn't have an entire section devoted to diet aids. Although over-the-counter diet aids may not be as dangerous as prescription drugs, they are not wise choices for permanent weight control.

Diet pills. Prescription diet pills that contain amphetamines are designed to reduce the appetite while they raise the metabolic rate. But research indicates that these pills help people lose only about 10 pounds (4.5 kg), and the weight is re-

Diet aids fill many drugstore counters.

gained even more quickly than if pills were not used.

Over-the-counter diet pills are believed to be safe for most healthy people. The active ingredient, which is also used as a decongestant in cold pills, depresses the brain's hunger center. But although dieters may lose more weight while using these pills than they would without them, researchers suggest that this loss only amounts to an extra 8 ounces (227 g) a week. And the pills do nothing to keep the weight off once the dieter stops taking them.

Diet candies and gums. These diet aids contain a mild anesthetic that numbs the taste buds. Promoters claim that this will make food less appealing so that less will be eaten. Although these may help those who eat mainly because they enjoy the taste of food, they probably have little effect on those who eat because they are hungry or for some psychological reason.

Fiber. Taking fiber pills is more likely to result in your losing your money rather than your weight. Swallowing the recommended fifteen or so pills every day provides about the same amount of fiber found in two inexpensive pieces of bread. The theory behind these pills is that they add bulk in the stomach so that you won't feel hungry. Natural fiber, such as pectin in apples, does seem to have slight weight-reducing properties. And some high-fiber foods, such as air-popped popcorn, are great for filling you up for very few calories. But fiber pills sold as aids in weight loss are probably a waste of money.

Another high-fiber theory suggests that adding bran to your daily diet will make you feel full and less likely to overeat. It also claims that the added fiber will make the food pass through the intestines faster so that fewer calories will have time to be absorbed. There is no proof that this works. In addition, too much fiber can make it harder for the body to absorb some important minerals. Although increasing natural fibers by eating more fruits, vegetables, and grains is certainly a healthy move, sprinkling fiber over everything you eat in an attempt to lose weight may do more harm than good.

Water pills. Diuretics, which increase the secretion of urine, are popular among high school and college wrestlers who want to lose weight quickly. Since the lost weight is only water, it's regained almost immediately. The regular use of diuretics may pose a danger of heart damage and the loss of important minerals such as potassium.

Thyroid hormones. Some weight-loss clinics claim that they will help you lose weight by raising your body's metabolic rate with thyroid hormones. Although the metabolic rate does go up, the thyroid hormone makes the body burn more of its lean body mass than fat. This can be extremely dangerous, as it may have a bad effect on the heart. Taking extra thyroid hormones may suppress normal production of the hormone in the body. As with other diet methods, the weight is quickly regained when the medication stops. Having to continue taking the medication for the rest of your life would be far more dangerous than being over-weight. Thyroid hormone treatment should only be administered by a qualified doctor.

LOSING WEIGHT SENSIBLY

The problem with most diets is that they are more concerned with short-term weight loss than with lifetime weight control. Going on a temporary diet may take weight off, but it is only by changing basic eating and lifestyle patterns that permanent weight loss can be achieved. You shouldn't do anything to lose weight that you aren't willing to do to keep it off.

Quite simply, losing weight is accomplished by using up more energy (calories) than you take in through food. This means either eating less or exercising more, or a combination of the two. Unfortunately, this is not always easy to put into practice. The following suggestions might help.

1. *Set realistic goals.* Setting impossible goals insures failure. Aim for a weight you can be happy with, not an unrealistic one that is beyond the bounds of your genetic legacy. Aim for a moderate weight loss of 1 or 2 pounds (.45 to .90 kg) a week. Research has shown that losses greater than this tend to be in the form of water and lean muscle mass rather than fat.

2. *Choose a sensible eating plan.* Don't fall for gimmicky diets. Choose one that is balanced, with foods from all food groups. The best diets are low in fats and high in complex carbohydrates. Limit intake of fats, sweets, and high-calorie foods.

3. *Don't be in a hurry.* Studies have shown that in most cases, the faster people lose weight, the more likely they are to regain it. The secret of success is to lose weight slowly, not more than 1 or 2 pounds (.45 or .90 kg) a week.

4. *Exercise.* Exercise not only burns calories, it gets those calories from the fat you want to lose and not from muscle. Muscle tissue is among the first to go when you lose weight by diet alone. Exercise can also speed up the rate that your body uses calories even after the exercise session is over. Regular exercise has been shown to reduce the appetite.

EATING DISORDERS: WHEN WEIGHT CONSCIOUSNESS IS EXTREME

Anorexia Nervosa

Patients with anorexia nervosa are so afraid of getting fat that they literally starve themselves. Ninety-five percent of anorexics are girls, mostly white girls from the middle or upper income brackets. Most of the girls were outstanding children who were eager to please and did excep-

*This girl, suffering from anorexia nervosa,
is probably thinking as she looks at herself
in the mirror that she is too fat.*

tionally well in school. In spite of their accomplishments, they tend to have low self-esteem and are driven to overachieve. They feel helpless and unable to change anything in their lives. Starving themselves seems to be the only way for them to get control.

Anorexics have a very distorted body image. They think they are fat, even after losing up to 25 percent of their body weight. Their one consuming interest is in becoming thin by eating very little and exercising to the point of exhaustion. Usually, the girls stop having their menstrual periods. Up to 20 percent of anorexics may die from the effects of starvation or from suicide.

Treatment for anorexia nervosa begins with medical assistance in helping the girl gain weight. Then individual and family therapy is needed to help the patient develop a better self-awareness and to eliminate any problems in the home that may have been involved in bringing on the condition. For permanent recovery, patients must develop positive feelings toward their bodies and a desire to be healthy.

Bulimia
Bulimia is an eating disorder characterized by binge eating, followed by purging through vomiting, laxatives, diuretics, and radical diets. Like anorexia nervosa, bulimia is found mostly in adolescent girls concerned about their weight and who have a fear of not being able to stop eating voluntarily. Many of them go on stringent diets, then

secretly binge by eating tremendous amounts of food within an hour or two. They then get rid of the food by vomiting or using laxatives. Bulimics realize that their behavior is abnormal, and this makes them depressed and disgusted with themselves.

Unlike anorexics, bulimics are not terribly thin. They are more apt to be of normal weight or even slightly above normal. However, this weight fluctuates over short periods by as much as 10 pounds (4.5 kg).

There are many dangerous health problems related to bulimia. Teeth and gums may become decayed from the acid brought up by vomiting. Frequent vomiting can also cause tears or ruptures to the esophagus. Excessive use of laxatives and diuretics can cause dehydration and other electrolyte disturbances and may involve disorders of the heart and kidney. Ultimately, these could cause seizures and even death.

Medical help is needed to interrupt the cycle of overeating and purging. Therapy is used to help the patient deal with the psychological problems of the condition.

Today's society is contributing to the increased incidence of eating disorders. Too much emphasis is placed on thinness and material success instead of emphasizing personal success and self-esteem. It is important for parents to push weight control only for health reasons, not for fashion. It is also important for parents and teachers to be aware of the signs of eating disorders. These include sudden or severe weight loss or gain; frequent fluctuation of weight; food hoarding; skipping meals or fasting; frequent nausea, bloating, or constipation; abnormal use of laxatives or diuretics; exaggerated fear of gaining weight; amenorrhea (stoppage of menstrual periods); and loss of dental enamel caused by frequent vomiting. The sooner these disorders can be detected, the better the chances are that the girl can recover completely.

SIX

THE EXERCISE CONNECTION

If you heard an advertisement for something that would get rid of your fat, give you energy, make you strong, make you feel younger, and protect you from various diseases, you might think it was just another outlandish claim thought up by someone trying to get rich. But there is something that provides all those benefits and doesn't need to cost anything. It's exercise. Exercise is nutrition in action. It not only affects the amount of food you can eat, it also enhances the body's ability to make the most of the nutrients you take in.

At one time it was believed that too much exercise would wear the body out. Now we know that the opposite is true. Exercise makes demands on the various body systems, giving them a chance to work at their peak level. Unfortunately, exercise is seen by many as something requiring pain, sweat, and hard work. But now we know that even moderate, enjoyable exercise can add tremendous benefits to a person's life.

TYPES OF EXERCISE

Exercise can be divided into those types that use oxygen (aerobic) and those that do not (anaerobic). There are two popular types of anaerobic exercises. Isometrics contract the muscles without moving the joints or limbs. A typical isometric exercise would be to contract your biceps for ten or twenty seconds, then relax. When a muscle is contracted and then a joint, limb, or both are moved, as in weightlifting and calisthenics, the exercise is called isotonic. Isometric and isotonic exercises are beneficial in increasing the strength, size, and tone of the muscles, but they have little or no effect on the cardiovascular system. Since these exercises may cause a brief rise in blood pressure, they could be dangerous for people with hypertension or other cardiac risks.

Aerobic exercises, such as brisk walking, jogging, swimming, biking, and so on, make the heart beat faster over a sustained period of time. They condition the heart so that it beats stronger and steadier, requiring fewer strokes to pump the same amount of blood. Blood pressure and pulse rate are lowered. As breathing becomes deeper, the capacity of the lungs increase. Circulation improves as more oxygen is taken in and the number and size of blood vessels increases. With more oxygen reaching all parts of the body, the individ-

ual has more endurance during strenuous physical activities. Aerobic exercises are also good fat burners.

EXERCISE IN
WEIGHT CONTROL

The main reason too many Americans are overweight is that we are more sedentary than evolution intended us to be. Our bodies were built for action, and they do not function as well at low levels of activity.

A sedentary life-style makes it easy for the body to accumulate extra pounds. When this happens, most people react by going on a diet. But up to 95 percent of the people who lose weight on diets gain it back. These depressing statistics would not be so high if dieters would include exercise as part of their weight-loss strategy.

Exercise, especially the aerobic type, not only burns calories, it can affect the body's metabolic rate, which involves the rate at which calories are

Jogging is an excellent aerobic exercise. However, runners must be careful to wear the proper shoes and to "warm up" before starting to run.

burned. Vigorous exercise not only raises the metabolic rate, it also keeps the rate up so that your body continues to use extra calories for up to fifteen hours after you stop exercising. Recent studies at Cornell University showed that this rise in metabolic rate is even greater when you exercise within two or three hours after eating. It appears that exercise at these times uses up more calories than the same exercise done on an empty stomach.

Exercise also increases the amount of lean tissue in the body and reduces the amount of fat. Lean tissue has a higher metabolic rate and takes more calories to maintain than fat tissue. Therefore, the more muscle you have, the more tissue you have that burns calories at an elevated rate. This is one reason it is foolish to go on quick weight-loss diets that reduce the amount of fat-burning muscle while leaving the fat itself behind.

Today, the proportion of fat to lean body mass (muscle, bone, organs, and tissue) is one factor in determining fitness. Two people may be the same height and weight but have very different body compositions. The person whose body is 15 percent fat is considered more fit than one whose body is 35 percent fat. Experts say that women should have about 20 percent body fat, while men should have about 15 percent. Fat levels of more than 30 percent for women and more than 25 percent for men are considered unhealthy. Using body composition to determine fitness has an advantage over the standard height-weight tables because it distinguishes between "overweight" and "overfat."

The percentage of body fat can be determined by a variety of methods, including underwater weighing and skinfold thickness measurements. These must be performed by a trained person who can administer the test and make the correct calculations. An easy self-test you can do is to pinch the thickness of the fat folds at your waist and abdomen, making sure that no muscle is included. If you can pinch an inch or more of fat, chances are you have too much body fat.

Although exercising will reduce the amount of fat in the body, spot reducing, or overexercising a certain area to lose fat there, will not work. Doing a hundred situps or leg lifts every day will help strengthen and firm the muscles of the abdomen or thighs, but it will not get rid of the blob of ugly fat sitting on top of those muscles. Equally ineffective are devices such as "Belly Busters" and elastic loops, or weights, that promise to get rid of flabby thighs, hips, abdomens, and waists.

The reason spot reducing doesn't work is that the fat sitting on top of muscles is merely being stored there for use by the entire body. It will only be used when the body has to dip into its fat reserves to supply the energy it needs. Using just one muscle to try to get rid of fat will take much longer than using a lot of muscles, as in aerobic exercises. Dieting and exercise together can lower the overall fat stores.

EXERCISE AND
HEART DISEASE

The heart is a muscle, and like all muscles, the stronger and healthier it is, the more efficiently it will work. Aerobic exercise improves muscle tone and increases muscle mass, so the heart becomes stronger and better able to withstand stress. This makes the heart more resistant to a heart attack. If a heart attack should occur, it is less likely to be fatal. Studies have shown that regular exercise can lower the pulse rate and blood pressure somewhat. Some experts think that regular aerobic exercise even increases the size and number of vessels carrying blood to the heart. These could serve as "emergency routes" if the main vessels become clogged. Exercise may also widen the existing coronary arteries, making narrowing less of a problem.

Aerobic exercise reduces the risks of atherosclerosis (hardening of the arteries) by raising the level of HDLs, the so-called "good" cholesterol, in the blood. At first, it was thought that only long-

This high school class is obviously enjoying its aerobic workout, which can be done to music to help liven the session.

distance, endurance-type running had any significant effect on HDL levels. Now we know that even moderate exercise, done on a regular basis, may both lower levels of LDL, the "bad" cholesterol, and raise HDL levels in the blood.

Not only is exercise good for the heart, but *not* exercising is bad for it. A report published by the Centers for Disease Control in Atlanta says that a lack of exercise is at least as heart-risky as smoking a pack of cigarettes a day, having high blood pressure, or even having a high level of serum cholesterol.

EXERCISE AND DIABETES MELLITUS

Exercise is important in both types of diabetes mellitus. Individuals with insulin-dependent diabetes must be more careful about vigorous exercise and exercise only when their diabetes is well under control. They also need to discuss their exercise plans with their doctors. But with proper care, people with diabetes can take part in sports and other vigorous activities. This is important for their emotional as well as physical development.

Exercise is especially beneficial to people with non-insulin dependent, or adult-onset, diabetes. Since most of these people are overweight, exercise can help them burn off unwanted calories. More importantly, exercise can increase the body's ability to use the insulin it has. Through exercise, cells can actually regain some of the sensitivity to insulin that they had lost. Exercise does this by making insulin receptors on the surface of cells more available. It may also increase the number of these receptors. Studies have shown that exercise can have dramatic effects in improving control of blood sugar levels even in people over fifty.

EXERCISE AND OSTEOPOROSIS

Exercise is important in preventing osteoporosis, or "porous bones." The body will not build bone it doesn't need. Engaging in weight-bearing exercises, such as walking or jogging (but not swimming), lets the body know that more bone is needed. The body responds by sending more calcium to the bones to increase density.

Just as exercise will increase bone strength and density, the lack of exercise can decrease it. When patients must spend long periods of time in bed, their bones can lose calcium, which is never replaced. This is also a problem for astronauts who work in space because there is no gravity to put the needed stress on their bones.

EXERCISE AND HYPERTENSION

Hypertension, or high blood pressure, adds to the workload of the heart and arteries. The heart must

pump with more force, and the arteries must carry blood that is moving under greater pressure. The end result could be a heart attack or stroke.

Over a period of time, consistent aerobic exercise can reduce the heart rate and blood pressure. This often allows patients to reduce or even eliminate the need for medication. Exercise can also help patients lose weight, a common problem among those with hypertension. Even when no weight is lost, aerobic exercise may help lower blood levels of stress hormones that contribute to hypertension.

Although some exercise programs are good for people with high blood pressure, others can be dangerous. Weight lifting, isometrics, wrestling, and even some aerobic exercises, such as the use of a rowing machine, can give blood pressure a short but intense boost. These exercises should be avoided by those with hypertension.

PSYCHOLOGICAL BENEFITS OF EXERCISE

Most people know about the physical benefits of exercise, but now we know that exercise offers

Bicycling is a wonderful exercise aerobically and for building and strengthening bone.

many psychological benefits as well. Aerobic exercise has been shown to be a natural relaxant that can reduce anxiety and depression. These good feelings most likely come from a natural tranquilizing chemical, beta-endorphin, that is released in the brain during exercise. Exercise also provides a healthy release for anger and frustration. As individuals become more fit, their body image changes, increasing self-confidence.

NUTRITION FOR ATHLETES

Since muscle is made up mostly of protein, people used to think that eating high-protein diets would build more muscle. Now we know that this is not true. Muscles only grow when they are made to work harder. This encourages them to take up more protein. So although it is important for athletes to get enough protein in their diet, eating more than needed offers no benefit. The normal American diet already contains twice as much protein as the body needs to replace muscle tissue, and athletes, since they normally eat more, should have no problem meeting their protein needs. Many experiments have shown that adding extra protein to the diet does nothing to increase an athlete's strength, endurance, or speed. In fact, an excess of protein eaten over a long period of time may interfere with calcium metabolism and put an extra strain on the kidneys.

Proteins are not an important source of energy during exercise. The type of fuel the body uses differs for varying types of activity. During moderate exercise such as brisk walking, fat provides most of the energy. As the exercise becomes more intense and lasts longer, carbohydrates become the major fuel. At the maximum level, carbohydrates become the exclusive source of energy. Carbohydrates, which used to be thought of as fattening, have become the principal source of fuel during training and performance.

There is an important relationship between the amount of glycogen (stored carbohydrate) in the muscles and an athlete's endurance. The more glycogen the athlete has in his or her muscles at the beginning of a race, the longer he or she can last. Some athletes, such as marathon runners or long-distance cyclists, use a technique called "carbo-loading" to trick their muscles into storing more glycogen than normal.

The carbo-loading regimen begins about six days before an event. First, the body's glycogen stores are depleted through three days of rigorous training combined with a low-carbohydrate diet. For the next three days, the training tapers off, and a high-carbohydrate diet is begun. The result is a higher level of glycogen in the muscles and liver, which can increase the length of time an athlete can sustain his or her maximum performance. Carbo-loading is of little benefit for endurance events that last less than an hour.

Carbo-loading has its risks and disadvantages. Since water can be deposited in the muscle along with glycogen, the muscles can feel heavy

Athletes need a ready source of energy, for quick spurts of action. Protein, surprisingly, is not an important source of energy for this.

and stiff, which might reduce their efficiency. Even more serious, some older marathon runners have experienced cardiac (heart) pain and abnormalities. Many athletes feel that the side effects aren't worth the slight edge carbo-loading might give them. A simple high-carbohydrate diet would offer gains without the risks.

If carbo-loading is used at all, it should be carried out only with expert supervision. Because of its effects on the heart, it should not be done more than two or three times a year. It should not be used by children or adolescents, nor by those with diabetes or high fat levels in their blood.

It has been suggested that caffeine will also increase the amount of fuel used by athletes in an event. Caffeine helps the muscles conserve their glycogen by mobilizing free fatty acids. As a result, muscles burn more fat and less glucose. However, caffeine is a diuretic that will draw water down the urinary tract. It may be better to pass up the caffeine and save the water. Just the excitement of a race will stimulate enough increased adrenaline to mobilize the free fatty acids.

Water is extremely important during long periods of rigorous exercise. Among other functions, water serves to regulate body temperature. Excessive losses of body fluid could reduce muscle strength and make the heart less efficient. Water should be taken before, during, and after exercise.

Despite what advertisers say, it is not necessary to drink "sweat replacement" drinks such as Gatorade during or after strenuous exercise. These drinks, which contain sodium and potassium, offer no particular advantage over plain water because water is what needs replacing. In fact, these beverages tend to dehydrate the athlete before rehydrating can take place. The minerals lost in sweating are not hard to replace with food and don't have to be replaced right away. Those who drink large amounts of these beverages should make sure they drink enough water to eliminate the excess sodium.

The best way to build muscles is through proper training and good nutrition. Unfortunately, many athletes, both amateur and professional, adopt dangerous practices in an attempt to build their muscles faster. One dangerous practice is the use of anabolic steroids. This drug became newsworthy during the 1988 Olympic Games when gold-medalist runner Ben Johnson had to give up his medal when it was found that he had been taking steroids.

There is good reason for discouraging the use of anabolic steroids. Although they may help build muscle, the permanent damage they can do far outweighs their benefits. Younger athletes may never reach their full potential height because the bones of the lower back may fuse and terminate growth early. Possible immediate effects of using steroids include acne, sexual dysfunction, and uncontrollable fits of temper, called "roid rages." Long-term side effects may include early heart disease and liver tumors. Women who take steroids take on "masculine" characteristics. Some of them never return to normal.

There are no special foods or supplements that can take the place of a balanced diet and hard work when it comes to increasing athletic prowess. Protein supplements and megadoses of vitamins have never been shown to be of any special benefit to athletes, or anyone else for that matter. Exotic foods, such as bee pollen or ginseng root, benefit only those who profit from their sale. If any of the substances advertised as giving unusual benefits to athletes seem to work, it is only through the placebo effect. That is, if the person believes strongly that the products will improve performance, they just might.

SETTING UP
AN EXERCISE PROGRAM

Exercise programs may be hard to begin, but once they are established the benefits will provide the incentive to keep going. The exercise habit offers benefits to people of all ages. Children who are active are less likely to get fat from spending too much time snacking in front of the television. This is significant because obese children have a much greater chance of becoming obese adults.

Sports help adolescents develop more self-confidence and a better self-image. Exercise helps control weight and builds muscle mass. Adults of all ages can use exercise to counteract the slow-down in metabolism that often comes with advancing years. Exercise can keep weight and the percentage of body fat low and can prevent or reverse the "middle-age spread." Exercise in-

*Exotic foods, such as many of those
found in health food stores, generally
benefit only those who are selling them.*

creases strength and energy, allowing adults to be more active.

Exercise is also beneficial for senior citizens. The President's Council on Physical Fitness and Sports has said that with regular exercise, even senior citizens can turn the clock back ten to twenty years in terms of their fitness levels.

An exercise program should fit the specific needs of an individual. Those over age forty, and anyone with a chronic condition such as hypertension, diabetes, heart irregularities, and so on, should consult his or her physician before embarking on any exercise program.

Aerobic exercises are best for overall conditioning. To be considered aerobic, the exercise must raise the heart rate to between 70 and 85 percent of its maximum. You can figure your maximum heart rate by subtracting your age from 220. Then figure out what both 70 and 85 percent of that number would be. That gives you a range to work within. As you get in better condition, it will take more exercise to push yourself to that 70 to 85 percent range.

Choose an aerobic exercise that you enjoy doing. Jogging, cycling, swimming, cross-country skiing, aerobic dancing, and brisk walking are all aerobic. Handball, tennis, squash, and volleyball are not aerobic the way most people play them because there is too much stopping and starting. Golf and bowling are not aerobic for anyone. For nonathletic adults, low- to moderate-intensity activities should be chosen but performed for a longer period of time. The most popular exercise for adults in the United States is walking.

Aerobic exercises should be done for at least twenty to thirty minutes a minimum of three times a week. However, studies have shown that four or five thirty-minute sessions a week can be three times as effective and take off three times as much weight. You can get into shape faster by exercising longer, not harder. The catch is, exercise must become a *permanent* part of your life-style. Once regular exercise is stopped, your body will begin to lose muscle and gain fat, even if your weight stays the same.

The longer and harder you use your muscles, the more calories you will burn up. Therefore, it is helpful to incorporate more exercise into your daily routines. Any time you walk somewhere instead of ride, or take the stairs instead of the elevator, you are burning up calories and building up your muscles. By putting more activity into your life, you will get more out of it.

═══════SEVEN═══════

SWEETNERS AND CAFFEINE —
GOOD OR BAD?

Some of the products we enjoy the most are among the most controversial. Is sugar a villain, causing everything from heart disease to cancer, or is it safe for the average person? Does replacing sugar with artificial sweeteners help you lose weight or does it give you cancer? Does the caffeine in coffee and cola lead to birth defects and heart disease, or does it give you a lift to help you get more done? The answers are not all in yet, but recent evidence indicates that when consumed in moderation, these substances are not harmful to the average person.

SUGAR

The battle lines have been drawn in the sugar controversy. On one side are some nutritionists who feel that since sugar represents empty calories, it should be eliminated as much as possible from the diet. They say it is found in fattening foods and thus leads to obesity, diabetes, and heart disease if consumed in large amounts. But scientists at the Federal Drug Administration (FDA) reviewed over a thousand research papers and concluded that a normal amount of sugar, up to 18 percent of daily calories, is not harmful.

Sugar has perhaps been unfairly blamed for causing obesity. Studying the populations in many countries has shown that the rate of obesity rises as sugar consumption increases. But a closer look shows that where sugar consumption increases, usually fat and total calories consumed also rise. Most nutritionists now believe that obesity is not caused by sugar alone but by taking in too many calories from all foods. Consuming too much fat is much more likely to contribute to obesity than consuming an excess of sugar. It is not the sugar but the fat in sweet treats such as cookies, pies, and ice cream that makes them fattening.

Sugar has also been blamed for contributing to heart disease and diabetes. But each of these diseases is also affected by obesity, so it is more likely that it is the obesity that is to blame, not the sugar itself. High rates of diabetes and heart disease have not been reported in any society where obesity is rare.

Some researchers have claimed that sugar causes hyperactivity in children. One of these claims was based on the observation that children are more restless than usual on the day after Halloween. However, it is unscientific to say that this restlessness is caused by the sugar the children consume in their Halloween candy. The restlessness is just as likely to come from the excitement of the previous night.

Not only does sugar not cause hyperactivity, it may actually have a calming effect. It is now believed that carbohydrates increase the brain's supply of serotonin, a chemical messenger that encourages sleep. If this is true, sugar would be more likely to calm youngsters than to overexcite them. This theory has been supported by clinical tests.

Sugar has also been blamed for violent behavior. In the "Twinkie defense" case the jury was convinced that the man who killed a San Francisco mayor did so because of violence caused by eating too much sugar. However, because of the calming effect of sugar, research shows that it is not likely to cause violence.

TYPES OF NUTRITIVE SWEETENERS

The type of sweetener most often at the center of controversy is plain white table sugar, chemically named sucrose. But sugars, syrups, molasses, sugar alcohols, and honey are all nutritive sweeteners and all provide 4 calories per gram. In order to be used by the body, all types of sugar are converted to glucose. The human body doesn't care what source its sugar comes from. Still, some people insist that some types of sugar, such as "raw sugar" or fructose, are healthier.

The raw sugar sold in health food stores is not true "raw sugar," which contains too many impurities to be sold in the United States. What most people think of as raw sugar is actually turbinado sugar, which is refined to remove the impurities and most, but not all, of the molasses.

Some people claim that fructose is superior to table sugar because it is found naturally in fruits. Fructose is somewhat sweeter than sucrose, so in some cases, less can be used to get the same level of sweetness. However, the difference doesn't amount to enough calories to be significant. The biggest difference is in cost, with fructose costing much more than sucrose.

Many people think that raw sugar and honey are more healthful than white sugar because of the minerals they contain. It is true that these sweeteners do contain some nutrients, but they are in such tiny amounts that it would be absurd to rely on any kind of sugar for its nutrients. One exception is blackstrap molasses, which does contain over 3 milligrams of iron per tablespoon.

Excessive amounts of anything can be unhealthy, and sugar is no exception. It should not take the place of more nutritionally dense foods but can be eaten along with them. And those who must reduce their intake of calories would do well to cut back on the sugar they eat. But eliminating sugar from the diet of the normal individual is not only unnecessary, it is almost impossible. The average American eats more than a hundred pounds of sugar and other sweeteners a year. Roughly 70 percent of the sweeteners we consume are added to our foods during processing.

Although sugar doesn't provide nutrients, it is not all bad. By making food taste better, it encourages us to eat a wider variety of foods, including those that are sour or bitter and that without sugar wouldn't be eaten otherwise. Growing children may need some sugar to meet their need for calories unless fat is increased, which is considered more harmful than sugar. Increasing starchy foods can add so much fiber to the diet that children feel full before they have met their energy needs.

For a teenage boy who eats as many as 4,000 calories a day to get all the energy he needs and who eats some very nutritious foods as part of these 4,000 calories, the "empty calories" of cola beverages will not hurt him. However, this may not be true for teenage girls, who may be eating only 1,200 calories a day or less. They cannot afford the empty calories and should eat the most nutrient-dense foods.

One claim against sugar is partially true. Sugar can contribute to tooth decay. However, it is not the amount of sugar that is eaten but rather how long that sugar stays on the teeth that is the determining factor in the formation of cavities. Also, other carbohydrates, such as starch, can be hard on teeth because much of the starch is rapidly converted to glucose by the saliva in the mouth.

Cavities begin forming when the mouth's bacteria manufacture weak acids from sugar and other carbohydrates. The organic acids they make can erode tooth enamel and lead to cavities. The longer the carbohydrates stay on the teeth, the longer these acids do their damage. Therefore, sticky snacks are more likely to cause tooth decay than sugar eaten with meals. It isn't only sugar that causes the problem.

ARTIFICIAL SWEETENERS

Nonnutritive sweeteners provide sweetness without calories. Saccharin has been used for nearly a hundred years as a sweetener for diabetics and later by those on reducing diets. However, in March 1977, the FDA banned saccharin because of experiments showing that it caused cancer of the bladder in rats and thus might present a threat to human beings. Diabetics and dieters were outraged by the ban, so the FDA allowed the sale of saccharin as an over-the-counter drug to be used as a tabletop sweetener. It is still used today but must be sold with a warning label.

Cyclamates were discovered in 1944. In the 1950s manufacturers found that by mixing ten parts cyclamate to one part saccharin they could obtain a product fifty-five times as sweet as sugar without the bitter aftertaste of saccharin alone. In

1970 the FDA put a total ban on cyclamates because studies showed they caused bladder tumors in rats. The earlier tests used a combination of saccharin and cyclamates and the saccharin may have been responsible for any carcinogenic effect shown in the animals. Recent studies fail to prove that cyclamates pose any real danger to humans. The ban is expected to be lifted in the very near future.

Xylitol, another sweetener that was being considered as a possible alternative to saccharin, has also been banned because it was found to cause cancer in animals.

The artificial sweetener most frequently used today is aspartame, a combination of two amino acids. Marketed under the name Nutrasweet™, it is two hundred times sweeter than sugar. Aspartame was heavily tested before it was allowed on the market.

Aspartame was approved for use in carbonated beverages in 1983. Some critics charged that it broke down and exposed consumers to excessive levels of methanol. But the FDA found that the exposure to methanol from the use of these drinks was well below the levels considered harmful. Other foods—including juices, fruits, and vegetables—exposed consumers to higher amounts of methanol without adverse effects.

Some people using aspartame may experience headaches and other mild discomforts, but these only happen to people with an unusual sensitivity to the product. At this time there are no known serious or widespread health consequences to those using products containing aspartame.

Although artificial sweeteners have no calories, there is still no evidence that they help people lose weight. Research suggests that diet foods and sodas are simply added to regular diets and do not replace high-calorie foods. The American Cancer Society did a study involving more than 78,000 older women and found that those who used sugar substitutes were *more* likely to gain weight than those who did not.

CAFFEINE

Caffeine is a stimulant drug found naturally in coffee, tea, chocolate, and kola nuts. It is added to colas, Dr. Pepper, some other soft drinks, and certain medications. People like caffeine for its "pick-me-up" effect. Studies indicate that it can prevent lapses of attention and improve the performance of physical tasks, especially those related to speed. It has not been found to improve intellectual performance.

Caffeine is a mildly addicting drug, but its stimulating effects are not reduced with long-term use. Caffeine continues to make the person feel alert and active even with daily consumption. Heavy coffee or cola drinkers may suffer withdrawal symptoms, mainly headaches, if they suddenly stop using these beverages. A gradual reduction in the amount of caffeine consumed, however, should pose no problems.

Although moderate amounts of caffeine are thought to be harmless, excessive amounts may produce symptoms of caffeinism, including insomnia, nervousness, anxiety, irritability, stomach irritation, diarrhea, and disturbances in heart rate and rhythms. Regular users, however, develop a tolerance to caffeine and rarely experience more than a brief boost in their metabolic rates.

The suspicion that caffeine raises the risk of cancer now appears to be groundless. However, there are still differences of opinion as to its relationship to heart disease. Neither the famous Framingham Study nor a study of 7,705 Japanese showed any correlation between coffee drinking and heart attack risk. Yet a study done with 1,100 male graduates of the Johns Hopkins medical school found that those graduates who drank more than five cups of coffee per day were two-and-a-half times more likely to develop heart disease than those who drank no coffee.

Some studies indicate that drinking coffee increases the amount of cholesterol in the blood. This may be because caffeine helps certain enzymes take body fat out of storage and move it into the bloodstream. When you need to burn fat for energy, this may be beneficial, which is why some endurance athletes use caffeine. But if you're not burning a lot of fat, your body has no special reason to mobilize fat stores, and doing so could be harmful.

In 1980, the FDA advised pregnant women to avoid drinking coffee because of studies linking caffeine to birth defects in rats. However, human studies have failed to show this connection. Two studies published in 1982 and 1983 found no notable difference in the number of birth defects among babies of mothers who drank at least four cups of coffee daily with those who consumed none at all.

Even though caffeine is not shown to cause birth defects, pregnant and nursing women would be wise to keep caffeine to a minimum. Unborn and newborn babies have a limited ability to metabolize the stimulant.

There used to be much publicity linking caffeine to the development of benign lumps in some women's breasts, a condition known as fibrocystic disease. However, further studies have found no connection. Studies have also shown no proof that a caffeine-restricted diet cures the signs and symptoms of this disease.

With the supposed harmful effects of caffeine being publicized, more people have turned to decaffeinated coffees and teas, but even these drinks have met with controversy. One chemical used, trichloroethylene (TCE), was shown to produce liver cancer in mice. Coffee manufacturers claimed that a person would have to drink 50 million cups of decaffeinated coffee a day to match the amount fed to the animals. But they took enough notice of the studies to change the decaffeinating process to eliminate the use of the questionable chemical.

People with ulcers would be wise to avoid drinking coffee because it stimulates stomach acids. But in light of recent research, there seems to be no good reason why healthy adults can't drink a few cups of coffee a day, or slightly more tea, soft drinks, chocolate milk, or cocoa. As in everything else, moderation makes good sense.

EIGHT

PRACTICAL THEORIES OR FALSE CLAIMS?

The public today is bombarded with half-truths and misleading ideas concerning nutrition. Many claim miraculous benefits from special vitamins, herbs, or foods. Others use scare tactics to influence consumers to buy products that are unnecessary and sometimes dangerous. Some advertisers purposely arouse concerns over health, then suggest a product that will take care of the problem. It is these false claims and promises that keep billions of dollars flowing into the health food and vitamin industries. The public needs to take a closer look at these claims.

Claim: Health foods are more nutritious than conventional foods. Some people believe that food bought in a health food store is somehow superior to food bought at the local supermarket. But there is no evidence that so-called "health foods" give any special health benefit to the users. They only benefit those who make huge profits from the sale of these products.

Shopping at these stores can be dangerous for those who use "health foods" as a substitute for medical attention. Some store operators play the role of doctor, diagnosing their customer's ailments, then prescribing special foods or pills to relieve the symptoms. For this service, customers may pay twice as much as they would for products bought at a grocery store. Those who substitute "miracle foods" or pills for competent medical care are taking unwise risks with their health.

Health foods are not only supposed to promote health; they are also advertised as being totally safe. However, many contain natural toxins. Herbal teas, for instance, contain several chemicals that have never been tested for safety. Raw milk has not been pasteurized, a process in which heat is used to kill microorganisms. Although certified raw milk must meet strict standards, the possibility still exists that it contains microorganisms that can cause disease.

Claim: Organically grown foods are superior to those grown by conventional means. The term "organic" has two meanings. Chemically speaking, organic merely means a substance containing carbon. This would include all food, whether from animal or vegetable sources. More commonly, when we refer to "organic" foods, we mean those that have been "organically grown"—without the use of chemical pesticides or fertilizers. They are

*Organically grown fruits and vegetables
usually taste and look the same as fruits
and vegetables grown by other means.
Are they safer because they are
grown without the use of pesticides?
The evidence so far—probably not.*

usually grown in soil fertilized by organic fertilizers, such as manure and compost (rotted vegetable matter and garbage).

Some people feel that since organic fertilizers come from living sources they are better at improving the soil and will produce more nutritious foods. But plants don't use organic matter. They take up inorganic minerals from the soil and carbon dioxide from the air. Once absorbed, plants can't tell the difference between the minerals it gets from organic fertilizers from those it gets from chemical fertilizers.

There are two advantages to natural fertilizers, but their benefits are ecological, not nutritional. First, natural fertilizers improve the quality of the soil by improving its texture. Second, organic material returned to the soil is recycled in a natural way and its creation doesn't require the energy needed to make chemical fertilizers.

One fear of chemical pesticides and fertilizers is that they are poisonous and leave undesirable residues on food. There is no evidence showing that consumers have ever been harmed by pesticides used correctly, although some accidental contamination has occurred. The residues are closely monitored by federal and state governments. Inspections with sensitive equipment have made produce bought in grocery stores as safe, and sometimes safer, than fruits and vegetables grown in your own backyard.

Eliminating the use of all pesticides could cause a drop in world food production because of the damage done by various insects. Insects multiply at a phenomenal rate, about 191 quadrillion offspring in a single summer. So far, efforts at using nonchemical means of insect control have not proven to be successful on a large scale. In times of rising food costs and potential food shortages, it would be unwise to abandon the use of chemical fertilizers and pesticides.

Claim: All food additives are harmful. Many people believe that anything added to natural food is potentially dangerous. Others worry about the names of chemicals they see on the lists of ingredients on food products. Some go as far as to recommend that you should never eat anything you can't pronounce. However, it's silly to worry about eating chemicals, because *all* foods are chemicals, and so are all additives, whether they come from nature or from a laboratory.

Chemicals are added to foods for specific reasons. Some additives, such as vitamins and minerals, are added to improve or boost the nutritional value of the food. Others are used to keep the food fresh longer. Several additives, such as colorings and flavorings, are used to make the food look and taste better. Still other additives help in the processing or preparation of the food. The most common additives are sugar, salt, and corn syrup. These three, plus citric acid, baking soda, vegetable colors, mustard, and pepper, account for more than 98 percent, by weight, of all food additives used in this country.

The use of additives is not new. Thousands of years ago, salt and nitrates were added to foods to preserve them. Today, certain additives retard the growth of mold on bread, keep fats from getting rancid, give ice cream its creamy texture, and provide strawberry Jell-O™ with its flavor and color.

Without additives, it would be impossible to produce food in one part of the world and have it survive processing, packaging, transportation over great distances, and many months of storage before it is consumed. Foolishly restricting the use of additives because of imagined danger would adversely affect the quality, safety, and cost of the food we eat.

The additives in our foods are strictly regulated by the FDA. They are as safe as science can make them. New additives are only cleared for use after extensive testing by experts. They are controlled far more carefully than nature controls the toxins it places in foods. People worried about additives and pollutants in food should eat a variety of foods to make sure they don't get too much of any one substance.

VITAMINS AND MINERALS

To some people, vitamins are believed to contain magical substances that provide health, energy, and cures for many diseases. Perhaps this view comes from history, when vitamins were first discovered and found to cure some of the diseases of that earlier day, such as scurvy, beriberi, and pellagra. In truth, the only diseases that can be cured by vitamins are those caused by a vitamin deficiency. Taking more than the body needs offers no additional benefit. Unfortunately, much of the public would rather believe those who promise miraculous benefits than specialists in nutrition. This has left the public with a distorted view of vitamins and what they can and cannot do.

Claim: Taking vitamins will give you energy. Neither vitamins nor minerals supply energy themselves, but they do help convert carbohydrates, fats, and proteins into energy. Therefore, taking vitamin and mineral pills will do nothing for your energy level if there are no fuel nutrients to break down. It is true that a deficiency in some vitamins may cause a lack of energy, but most Americans suffer no such deficiency. Generally, any increased energy coming from vitamin pills is a result of the placebo effect. People believe they will have more energy, so they do.

Claim: Vitamin A will improve vision, cure acne, and retard aging. Vitamin A is a popular vitamin that some say can improve vision for those working under artificial light, calm hyperactive children, cure warts, improve dry or wrinkled skin, cure ulcers and respiratory infections, delay heart disease, and retard aging. However, there is no scientific evidence that vitamin A can make a significant difference in most of these conditions. There are, though, two areas in which vitamin A

Vitamin and mineral supplements line the shelves of many supermarkets, drugstores, and health food stores. But it is still better, if possible, to get your vitamins and minerals through the foods you eat, to ensure an overall healthy diet.

may be useful—in reducing the risks of certain types of cancer and in the treatment of acne.

Studies indicate that a vitamin A deficiency can increase the risks of getting certain types of cancer. One important study found that men who consumed diets low in vitamin A had twice the lung cancer rates of those with high levels of the vitamin. Beta-carotene, an element that is converted by the body into vitamin A, seems to be the most beneficial. There is no evidence that vitamin A itself, or beta-carotene, has any effect on a cancer that has already formed.

Another area in which vitamin A has shown some benefits is in the treatment of some types of acne. However, the type of vitamin A used (retinoic acid) is not taken internally but is applied to the skin. Retinoic acid speeds up skin-cell production, causing new cells to push to the surface and clearing the skin of dead cells. More recently, it has been used to ease wrinkling in the sun-damaged skin of older people. Because of its side effects, including skin irritations, this form of vitamin A can only be sold by prescription.

Although adequate amounts of vitamin A are necessary, too much of it is toxic. Vitamin A is stored in the fatty tissues of the body, making it difficult for the body to rid itself of excessive amounts. People who have accumulated too much vitamin A show fatigue, lethargy, brittle nails, sparse hair, dry and scaly skin, abdominal pain, liver damage, and calcium loss from the bones. In extreme cases, toxicity may mimic the symptom of a brain tumor, with increased pressure inside the skull. However, vitamin A's toxicity depends on its form. Only retinol and the other varieties found in animal foods are capable of doing much harm. Carotenoids, the vegetable sources of vitamin A, don't seem to be toxic.

Claim: Vitamin D will lower blood cholesterol.
Vitamin D is another fat-soluble vitamin that can become toxic when excessive amounts are taken. It is used by the body to regulate calcium and phosphate. Some people claim that large doses will lower blood cholesterol, prevent or cure osteoporosis in the elderly, and strengthen bones. Although it is true that a lack of vitamin D in infants and children will give them weaker bones, resulting in a condition called rickets, taking more vitamin D than needed will not make the bones super strong.

Vitamin D in large quantities can be extremely toxic, causing calcium to deposit in tissues other than bone. If these calcium deposits form in the aorta, the heart's major artery, it could cause death. It is possible to receive an overdose of vitamin D with as little as four to five times the recommended daily intake. Most people get all the vitamin D they need in sunshine and vitamin D-fortified milk. Taking supplements is unnecessary and unwise.

Claim: Vitamin C will cure the common cold.
Vitamin C is America's most popular vitamin sup-

plement. Much of its popularity comes from the belief that it will prevent or cure the common cold. Although one study showed that people who took large doses of vitamin C for a year had milder colds, several other studies failed to show any difference in the number and severity of colds between people taking vitamin C supplements and those who did not.

Vitamin C does help wounds heal properly and protects the body against scurvy, a disease characterized by swollen, bleeding gums and loosened teeth. It also helps the body resist infections and promotes the absorption of iron. Vitamin C's use as an antioxidant may help fight against cancer-causing free radicals, but it can't cure cancer in patients who have the disease.

Although obtaining adequate amounts of vitamin C is important, taking megadoses is useless. Since vitamin C is water soluble, any excess is excreted in the urine.

Claim: Vitamin E will improve sexual performance and prevent aging. Many exaggerated claims have been made for vitamin E based on the effects it has had on rats in studies. But its use for humans is not as remarkable. Vitamin E acts as an antioxidant that helps to prevent oxygen from destroying other substances. But, contrary to the many claims made, vitamin E will do nothing to restore sexual potency, enhance athletic performance, or help resist heart attacks, muscular disorders, or the hot flashes of menopause. It won't lower cholesterol levels in the blood or prevent aging. Adding vitamin E to toilet soaps and cosmetics only adds to their price; it doesn't heal skin blemishes, soften dry skin, ease wrinkles, or give new life to aging skin. Numerous experiments have discredited these and similar claims.

Vitamin E is found in many foods, including vegetable oils, liver, beans, fruits, and vegetables. Since the body stores so much vitamin E in its fatty tissues, vitamin E deficiencies are rare except in premature babies. Self-medication with vitamin E supplements may be dangerous, especially when they take the place of appropriate diagnosis and treatment.

Now that more people are taking megadoses of vitamin E, its toxic effects are beginning to turn up, although most of them are minimal. Excessive amounts, about ten times the recommended levels, may disrupt hormonal activity, change levels of fat in the blood, keep white blood cells from doing their job, and interfere with blood clotting.

Claim: Special vitamin formulas will help you deal with the stresses of daily life. Some vitamin promoters have taken advantage of the public's concern over stress and have put together vitamin combinations advertised as "stress vitamins." But when nutritionists talk about the need for extra vitamins during times of stress, they are not talking about the psychological stress brought on by the pressures of careers, school, or emotional problems. They are referring to the physical stress brought on by illness, infection, or injury. During these times, the body's reserves of stress-fighting vitamins, namely vitamin C and some B vitamins, can be depleted. But increased doses of these vitamins are only needed during times of *extreme* physical stress—not for minor illnesses.

Even though these vitamins do nothing to reduce psychological stress, vitamin manufacturers still advertise special "stress formulas" with megadoses of vitamin C and some B vitamins, implying that they will help in dealing with the stresses of daily life.

Claim: Since vitamins are good for you, taking more of them is even better. Many people looking for optimum health treat themselves with vitamin megadoses, ten or more times the amount nutritionists recommend. At best, this is a foolish practice; at worst, it is dangerous. The body needs specific amounts of nutrients and has no use for excesses. In most cases, the excesses are excreted as waste, but some are stored in the body, occasionally reaching dangerously high levels. Even moderately high doses of some fat-soluble vitamins, such as vitamins A and D, are known to be toxic. Also, since nutrients are needed in proper proportions, taking large doses of one may throw off the balance of others.

Claim: Natural vitamins are better than synthetic vitamins. All vitamins are chemicals, and the body can't tell the difference between those from natural sources and those that are synthetic. The big difference is in price, with "natural" vitamins costing about twice as much. Taking either type of vitamin pill is not as beneficial as eating foods containing the vitamins, because foods have so many other fringe benefits, such as fiber, carbohydrates, and other vitamins and minerals.

Claim: Everyone should take vitamin supplements for "insurance." Some doctors think that taking a vitamin pill containing no more than 100 percent of the Recommended Dietary Allowances (RDAs) for all the micronutrients is good "insurance." Others consider it a waste of money. Most people get all the nutrients they need from a balanced diet. If they are not getting what they need from food, it would be far wiser to improve the diet rather than to rely on pills.

Vitamin and mineral supplements may be advisable for those who cannot meet their needs through diet alone. This may include the elderly and low-income families; people, especially women, who take in fewer than 1,500 calories a day, making it difficult for them to get all the vitamins they need; and pregnant or nursing mothers and their infants who have special nutritional needs. Others who run special risks of vitamin deficiencies are smokers, alcoholics, and patients with certain medical conditions. Women of childbearing age may need iron supplements to replace the iron lost through menstruation.

If a vitamin/mineral supplement is taken at all, it should be one supplying less, or certainly no more, than 100 percent of the U.S. Recommended

Daily Allowance of any nutrient. It may not be necessary to take a supplement every day. If the diet is fairly well balanced, taking a supplement once every two or three days is sufficient.

Claim: The right diet will make you live longer. This claim is true in one way and false in another. Eating properly can help prevent some of the diseases that make people die prematurely, but no diet will allow you to live longer than your genetic heritage dictates. Many more people are reaching old age today because of better medical care, which has eliminated many of the infectious diseases of earlier times. However, the maximum number of years humans can live has not changed that much. The maximum age an individual can reach is determined by heredity. Food choices—no matter how right they are—cannot extend the life span beyond that limit. However, good nutrition helps prolong the body's health and vigor into the later years.

A lifestyle that values healthy habits in all areas is important in making the best of later years. These habits include getting adequate sleep, eating regular meals, maintaining desirable weight, not smoking, getting regular exercise, and drinking alcohol moderately or not at all. These things are wise practices for any age.

Claim: Diet can cure hyperactivity. From 5 to 20 percent of American children, most of them boys, may be hyperactive. They are overly active, have short attention spans, and are impulsive. In 1975 a California pediatric allergist, Dr. Benjamin Feingold, theorized that hyperactivity was caused by food colorings and artificial flavorings, particularly those containing salicylate, the chemical found in aspirin. Although many parents tried Feingold's diet and believed that it worked for their children, extensive testing failed to prove his theory. The medical and behavioral scientists who reviewed the results of these studies found no instances of dramatic improvement when the children's diets were free of food colors and no drastic decline when the colors were added back to the diets. In most cases, any improvements that were reported appear to have come from the added attention the children received while they were on the diet.

Claim: Eating chocolate causes acne. The parents of many of today's teenagers remember their own teen years, when they were told that eating chocolate or drinking colas would result in pimples on their faces. Many foods were thought to cause or aggravate acne, including chocolate, cola beverages, fatty or greasy foods, milk, nuts, seafood, sugar, and salt containing iodine. But today, chocolate bars are off the hook, at least as far as acne is concerned. None of these foods has been shown to cause acne, and in only a very small percentage of cases does a particular food seem to aggravate acne.

No one knows exactly why some people get acne and others don't. Heredity may be involved, because acne tends to run in families. Also, the change in hormones associated with adolescence plays a role by increasing the activity of the glands in the skin. Although a healthy diet is necessary for overall health, particular foods cannot be singled out as the villains in acne.

KNOWING WHAT (AND WHO) TO BELIEVE

Since food fads and fallacies are always going to be with us, it is important to know how to evaluate the claims made. The most important tip is to consider the source. Does the background of the individual who is endorsing or promoting the product qualify that person to be giving advice? Is the person a member of a reputable nutrition organization (such as the American Dietetic Association or the American Institute of Nutrition), or of an appropriate related professional organization (such as the American Medical Association)? Are claims backed up with actual scientific proof or only anecdotes about how well the product or technique worked for certain people?

Consider what the individual making the claim has to gain. A doctor or nutritionist writing in a professional journal is a much more reliable source than someone trying to get rich by selling vitamins, diet products, or books making exaggerated promises.

Beware of claims promising great benefits for little or no effort. People can be especially gullible when they think they can get something for nothing, and they usually come out on the losing end. Be wary of anyone promising to "detoxify your body," "release your energy," "boost your immune system," or "balance your chemistry." These are all catch phrases used by people trying to get money from an unsuspecting public.

Consider whether or not the product or idea seems logical in light of what you already know about nutrition. Try to find additional documentation for all claims made.

Finally, consider the consequences of following the new idea or buying the new product. Is there a possible health hazard, or would you be spending money unwisely that you could better use for something else? A dose of basic nutritional knowledge and common sense will go a long way toward protecting you from being taken in by false claims and hoaxes.

─────*NINE*─────

KNOWLEDGE IS
NOT ENOUGH

Sorting through all the nutritional information, both proven and unproven, may seem so confusing that knowing how to put together a nutritious diet seems almost impossible. Yet mounting scientific evidence indicates that what you eat plays a significant role in the development or prevention of various diseases, including cancer, heart disease, obesity, osteoporosis, and high blood pressure. Also, your body can't function at peak levels if it isn't getting everything it needs.

Much of the food advice we get is confusing because the foods that reduce risks of developing one disease may increase the risks of developing another. For example, calcium-rich dairy products are good for the bones but often contain saturated fat and cholesterol that may contribute to heart disease. Red meats and eggs are excellent sources of protein and iron, yet they also contain the saturated fats and cholesterol that may lead to

"This food has a high endorsement from the American Heart Association, but it has a warning label from the National Cancer Institute."

atherosclerosis. Polyunsaturated fats may lower serum cholesterol levels, but at the same time they may increase the formation of free radicals that contribute to the development of cancer. How can you get a diet that is good for everything?

The main thing to do is relax. Some people become so worried about what they eat that they lose the enjoyment associated with food. The two main goals should be variety and moderation. From there you can make subtle changes to add to your diet those foods thought to reduce disease risk and cut back on the foods thought to raise those risks.

READING FOOD LABELS

Since so many of our foods are processed, the only way to know what we are getting is to read the labels. Most processed foods must have their ingredients listed on the labels. The list begins with the ingredient used in the largest amount by weight, followed by the other ingredients in descending order.

Lists of ingredients can be misleading. Some manufacturers list several sweeteners so that the product appears to contain less sugar than it really does. Sugar, dextrose, brown sugar, molasses, corn syrup, malt syrup, maple syrup, fructose, sucrose, and honey are all sources of sugar. Beware of anything ending in the letters *-ose*. That means sugar.

Nutritional information is required only if a manufacturer adds protein or one or more vitamins or minerals to the product, or if a nutritional claim is made on the label, such as "now contains fewer calories." But many manufacturers include nutritional information even on products that do not require it. The nutritional information includes the number of calories and the amount of protein, carbohydrates, fat, and sodium contained in each serving of the product. It may also include the amount of cholesterol, fatty acid, and potassium. In addition, under the heading "percentage of Recommended Daily Allowances," consumers are given the amounts of protein and seven essential vitamins and minerals in each serving.

The terms "cnriched" and "fortified" may appear on a label. "Enriched" refers to the addition of thiamin, riboflavin, niacin, and iron to bread, flour, and cereal products in amounts specified by law. Products labeled "fortified" contain the addition of one or more nutrients that were not present or were present in small amounts in the natural food. They include the addition of vitamins A and D to milk, iodine to salt, and iron to breakfast cereals.

The word "light" on the label tells you nothing specific about its caloric content. But a product marked "low-calorie" can, by FDA regulation, have no more than 40 calories per serving. Again, the FDA regulations require that a "reduced-calorie" food must have one-third fewer calories than it would in its standard form, or the phrase cannot be used on the label or in advertising.

RECOMMENDED DIETARY ALLOWANCES

For nearly half a century, the Food and Nutrition Board of the National Academy of Sciences has established nutritional and dietary guidelines. About every five years since 1943 the board has issued its Recommended Dietary Allowances (RDA), which set forth the recommended amounts of nutrients for infants, children, and grown men and women of various ages. From the RDAs, the Food and Drug Administration formulates its Recommended *Daily* Allowances, which give a single standard for each nutrient. They are meant to be adequate for anyone of any age and either sex.

Using the Recommended Daily Allowances would presumably ensure that you are getting all the nutrients you need, but they are too specific and too cumbersome for the average person to use. It would require finding the exact nutritional content of each food consumed, then adding up the figures to see if the recommended level of each nutrient had been met.

BASIC FOUR
FOOD GROUPS

In the 1950s, the USDA developed the Basic Four Food Groups, or just the Basic Four, which places foods of similar nutrient composition into groups. Two of the groups emphasize animal products and two emphasize plant products. By choosing the recommended number of daily servings from each group, an individual should be able to supply all the different nutrients needed continually in the diet. Recently, a fifth group was added to include fats, sweets, and alcohol, which all contain calories but very few nutrients.

Following the Basic Four encourages variety in the diet, but it doesn't guarantee a perfect diet. It does not protect against excesses. Even a diet high in fat, sugar, salt, and calories can meet the requirements of the guide. Still, it makes a good starting point in meal planning as long as other considerations are met.

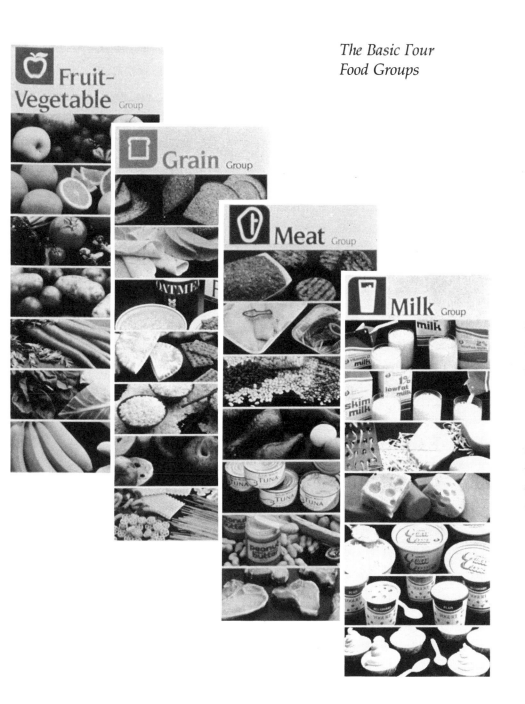

The Basic Four
Food Groups

The Basic Four Food Groups are: 1) the meat group, including poultry, fish, eggs, and legumes. Two or more servings are recommended; 2) milk and milk products, including cheese, yogurt, and ice cream. Two servings are recommended for adults, three or four servings for children; 3) vegetables and fruits. Four or more servings are recommended; and 4) breads and cereals, including whole grain and enriched grain products. Four servings are recommended. The extra group consists of sweets, fats, and alcohol and should only be used when essential nutrients are met and there is still room for more calories.

EATING HEALTHY

One problem with the tremendous amount of nutritional information available today is that it may cause the average consumer to focus on specific nutrients instead of focusing on the diet as a whole. It would almost take a mathematician to know whether or not you had exceeded the 300 mg limit on cholesterol recommended by the American Heart Association, or if only 30 percent of your calories came from fat with only 10 percent of those calories coming from saturated fat. Rather than aiming for specific percentages and amounts of nutrients, it makes more sense to follow some general guidelines, such as the following:

- Eat a variety of foods. There are about forty different nutrients needed by the body. It is impossible to get all of them without including a wide variety of foods in the diet.

- Avoid too much fat, saturated fat, and cholesterol. A high consumption of saturated fats and cholesterol has been associated with high levels of serum cholesterol in many people. Polyunsaturated and monounsaturated fats tend to lower blood cholesterol, but even these should be monitored because they have been linked with the formation of free radicals, which can lead to cancer. Too much fat in any form can lead to obesity and its related complications.
- Eat more complex carbohydrates and more fiber. Through the years, the average American diet has included reduced amounts of complex carbohydrates and fiber consumed and increased amounts of fat. A diet high in fruits, vegetables, and grains may reduce the risk of heart disease, diabetes, and some forms of cancer. These foods also add bulk to the diet and are helpful in weight control.
- Reduce the intake of salt. High intake of the sodium in salt has been associated with the development of hypertension (high blood pressure) in some people. Since most people eat up to ten times as much salt as needed, it won't hurt anyone to cut back some.
- Avoid too much sugar. Sugary foods not only promote tooth decay, they are often high in fat and calories and low in vitamins and minerals. Sugary foods can lead to obesity when they are eaten in excess.

- Maintain an "ideal" body weight. Excessive body weight has been shown to increase the risk of several chronic disorders, including high blood pressure, diabetes, and increased blood cholesterol.
- If you drink alcoholic beverages, do so in moderation. Excessive drinking can lead to many health problems, including cancers of the mouth, throat, esophagus, and liver. Cancer risk is especially high for heavy drinkers who smoke. Also, alcoholic drinks are high in calories and low in vitamins and minerals.

When taking dietary advice, it's good to follow the advice that fits you particularly. For instance, if your relatives have high blood pressure, watch your salt intake. If they have early heart and artery disease, control your intake of fat and cholesterol. If your parents are obese, watch your calorie intake and exercise regularly. One bit of advice that applies to all of us without exception is that we need to eat a balanced and varied diet and maintain moderation. If there's enough variety in your meals, and if you limit yourself to only occasional excesses, you're unlikely to do yourself much nutritional harm.

GLOSSARY

Aerobic exercise—Exercise performed at an intensity that causes oxygen intake and the transport of oxygen (breathing and heartbeat) to be speeded up.

Anabolic steroids—Hormones, produced normally in males during puberty, that bring about maturation. They are dangerous when used by athletes to try to promote muscular development.

Anaerobic exercises—Exercises that do *not* necessarily increase the body's use of oxygen.

Anemia—Any disease in which the size or shape of red blood cells is altered and their number is reduced.

Anorexia nervosa—An eating disorder characterized by self-starvation and weight loss to dangerous levels.

Antioxidant—A compound that protects other compounds from oxygen by reacting with the oxygen itself.

Atherosclerosis—A condition in which the inner lining of the arteries becomes thickened by deposits of fat, protein, cholesterol, and cell debris. Also called "hardening of the arteries."

Bulimia—An eating disorder characterized by periodic secret food binges followed by purging through vomiting, use of laxatives, and other extreme measures.

Carcinogen—A cancer-causing agent or substance.

Cholesterol—A fatlike substance that is required by every cell in the body and is synthesized in the body by the liver and taken in through foods of animal origin.

Coronary arteries—Arteries that supply blood to the heart muscle.

Diabetes mellitus—A disorder in which the body's ability to utilize carbohydrates is impaired because of inadequate production or poor utilization of the hormone insulin.

Diastolic pressure—Pressure within the blood vessels occurring when the heart rests between beats.

Diuretic—Any substance that increases the secretion of urine.

DNA—A nucleic acid found in cells that carries the genetic information of the cell.

Free radicals—Highly reactive compounds produced during oxidation; they can oxidize and destroy tissue in the body.

Glucose—Also known as blood sugar, it is the fuel preferred by the cells for energy and is derived mainly from carbohydrates in the diet.

Glycogen—The principal form in which carbohydrates are stored in animal tissue, primarily in the muscles and liver.

Hemoglobin—The oxygen-carrying iron-protein part of the blood, found in red blood cells.

Hydrogenation—The process of adding hydrogen to unsaturated fat to make it more solid and more resistant to chemical change.

Hypertension—High blood pressure.

Initiators—Cancer-causing substances that actually begin the process of abnormal cell growth.

Insulin—The hormone secreted by certain cells of the pancreas that is essential for proper metabolism of blood sugar.

Ketones—The collective term given to several intermediate products formed during the breakdown of fatty acids.

Lipoprotein—A combination of protein and fats. It is the form in which fat is carried through the bloodstream.

Megadoses—Quantities of a substance, such as a vitamin, that are massive compared to the amount required by the body.

Metabolic rate—The rate at which calories are used by the body to take care of basic needs such as breathing, heartbeat, tissue repair, body temperature, etc.

Neurotransmitter—A substance that serves as a chemical link for communication between nerve cells.

Obesity—A weight condition of more than 20 percent over desirable body weight due to excess body fat.

Osteoporosis—A condition in which there is a loss of bone over time, resulting in weakened bones that fracture easily.

Oxidation—The process in which substances are chemically combined with oxygen.

Peptic ulcer—An ulcer of the lining of the stomach or duodenum (upper segment of the small intestine).

Plaque—A mound of lipid material, smooth muscle cells, and calcium that accumulates in the inner artery wall, causing atherosclerosis.

Promoter—A substance that does not initiate cancer but gives the damaged cells a better chance of growing into a tumor.

Systolic pressure—Pressure within the blood vessels during contraction of the heart.

Triglycerides—Three fatty acids linked to a molecule of glycerol that make up the main form of fat found in body tissues and in food.

SOURCES USED

Alabaster, Oliver, M.D. *What You Can Do To Prevent Cancer.* New York: Simon & Schuster, 1985.

The American Heart Association Diet. Dallas: American Heart Association, 1985.

Bailey, Covert. *Fit or Fat?* Boston: Houghton Mifflin, 1978.

Burton, Benjamin T., and Willis R. Foster. *Human Nutrition.* New York: McGraw-Hill, 1988.

Campbell, T. Colin, and Thomas P. O'Connor. "Scientific Evidence and Explicit Health Claims in Food Advertisements," *Journal of Nutrition Education.* Vol. 20, No. 2, 1988.

Cassidy, Anne. "The New View on Hypertension," *Health Report.* New York: Whittle Communications, 1988.

Connor, Sonja L., and William E. Connor. *The New American Diet.* New York: Simon & Schuster, 1986.

Cooper, Dr. Kenneth H. *The Aerobics Program for Total Well-Being.* New York: M. Evans, 1982.

Diabetes Education Center. *Diabetes.* New York: Doubleday, 1984.

Ellenbogen, Leon. *Controversies in Nutrition.* New York: Churchill Livingston, 1981.

"Gambling with Your Heart," *Self.* March 1988.

Hamilton, Eva Nay Nunnelley, and Eleanor Noss Whitney. *Nutrition, Concepts and Controversies.* St. Paul, Minnesota: West Publishing, 1982.

The Heart and Blood Vessels. Dallas: American Heart Association, 1973.

High Blood Pressure. Dallas: American Heart Association, 1983.

Lake, Alice. "Dieting Can Make You Fat," *McCall's.* August 1988.

Lecos, Chris W. "Caffeine Jitters: Some Safety Questions Remain," *FDA Consumer.* (Reprint: Government Printing Office. HHS Publication No. [FDA] 88-2221.) December 1987/January 1988.

_____. "Planning a Diet for a Healthy Heart," *FDA Consumer.* (Reprint: Government Printing Office. HHS Publication No. [FDA] 87-2220.) March 1987.

_____. "Sweetness Minus Calories = Controversy," *FDA Consumer.* (Reprint: Government Printing Office. HHS Publication No. [FDA] 85-2205.) February 1985.

Lehmann, Phyllis. "More Than You Ever Thought You Would Know About Food Additives." *FDA Consumer.* (Reprint: Government Printing Office. HHS Publication No. [FDA] 82-2160.) February 1982.

Long, Patricia J., and Barbara Shannon. *Nutrition, an Inquiry into the Issues.* New Jersey: Prentice-Hall, 1983.

Omizo, Sharon A., and Ethel Aiko Oda. "Anorexia nervosa: Psychological considerations for nutrition counseling," *Journal of the American Dietetic Association.* Vol. 88, No. 1, January 1988.

President's Council on Physical Fitness and Sports. *Exercise and Weight Control.* U.S. Department of Health & Human Services, The President's Council on Physical Fitness and Sports. Washington D.C., no date.

Rock, Cheryl L., and Ann M. Coulston. "Weight-control approaches: A review by the California Dietetic Association." *Journal of the American Dietetic Association.* Vol. 88, No. 1, January 1988.

Saltman, Paul, Joel Gurin, and Ira Mothner. *The California Nutrition Book.* Boston: Little, Brown, 1987.

"Some Facts and Myths of Vitamins." *FDA Consumer.* (Reprint: Government Printing Office. HHS Publication No. [FDA] 79-2117). September 1979.

Sorenson, Ann W., Martha L. Slattery, and Marilyn H. Ford. "Calcium and Colon Cancer: A Review," *Nutrition and Cancer.* Vol. II, No. 3, 1988.

Stare, Fredrick J., and Margaret McWilliams. *Living Nutrition.* New York: John Wiley & Sons, 1984.

Trafford, Abigail. "America's Diet Wars," *U.S. News & World Report.* Vol. 100. January 20, 1986.

U.S. Department of Health and Human Services. *Anabolic Steroids, Losing at Winning.* U.S. Department of Health and Human Services, Public Health Service, Food and Drug Administration. Government Printing Office (DHHS Publication No. [FDA] 88-3171).

_____. *Diet, Nutrition & Cancer Prevention: a guide to food choices.* U.S. Department of Health and Human Services, Public Health Service, National Institutes of Health. Washington D.C.: Government Printing Office (NIH Publication No. 85-2711). 1984.

_____. *Eating to Lower Your High Blood Cholesterol.* U.S. Department of Health and Human Services, Public Health Service, National Institutes of Health. Washington D.C.: Government Printing Office (NIH Publication No. 87-2920). 1987.

Whelan, Dr. Elizabeth M., and Dr. Fredrick J. Stare. *The 100% Hoax.* New York: Atheneum, 1983.

Willis, Judith. "How To Take Weight Off (And Keep It Off) Without Getting Ripped Off," *FDA Consumer* (Reprint: Government Printing Office, HHS Publication No. [FDA] 85-1116). February 1985.

Winick, Myron. *Nutrition and Exercise.* New York: John Wiley & Sons, 1986.

FOR FURTHER READING

Bailey, Covert. *Fit or Fat?* Boston: Houghton Mifflin, 1978.

Lukes, Bonnie L. *How to be a Reasonably Thin Teenage Girl.* New York: Atheneum, 1986.

Lyttle, Richard B. *The New Physical Fitness.* New York: Franklin Watts, 1981.

Perl, Lila. *Junk Food, Fast Food, Health Food.* New York: Houghton Mifflin/Clarion Books, 1980.

Thompson, Paul. *Nutrition.* New York: Franklin Watts, 1981.

Whelan, Elizabeth M., and Fredrick J. Stare. *The 100% Hoax.* New York: Atheneum, 1983.

INDEX